Christian Leadership in the Professional World

Where Biblical Wisdom Meets the Corner Office

Justin Wilson

Contents

By the Grace of God, They Aligned

For most of my adult life, I had no room for God. I grew up with religion, some exposure to Mormonism and Christianity through my parents who chose different faiths, but I walked away from all of it at sixteen when I started working. I scheduled myself on Sundays specifically to avoid church. By the time I moved to Texas in 2007 to start my career in tech, I was done with faith.

I married a Christian woman. She took me to church and I went, physically, but I was rarely there mentally. For over 10 years, I sat in those chairs rubbing my wife's back, thinking about the NFL, video games, work problems, anything but God. I had a career to build, problems to solve, and no interest in ancient books about things I couldn't see or measure and the answer was just have faith.

I spent about twelve years as a software developer, then moved into system architecture and became a chief architect. Recently, I became a CTO. My entire career has been in tech. Code, systems, results. If something couldn't be tested, debugged, and proven, I didn't have time for it, but I did have bad bosses. Bosses who hacked into my email to see if I was job hunting. Bosses who yelled constantly and thought their terrible ideas were gold. Bosses who worked from home while requiring everyone else on-site. Bosses who promised confidentiality, then betrayed it fifteen minutes later. Those bad bosses taught me something more valuable than any MBA program could have: they taught me exactly what not to do.

Over the next several years, starting around 2016, through trial and error, through making mistakes and having to clean up the wreckage, through crisis after crisis that forced me to figure out what actually works when the stakes are real, I built a framework. I didn't set out to build a philosophy. I just needed a way to make decisions about people and problems that didn't destroy trust the way I'd watched my bosses destroy mine. I needed principles that would hold when the pressure was on and everyone was watching.

So I asked myself questions:

- *Have I ever made the mistake this person just made?* (Because if I had, who was I to judge them more harshly than I'd want to be judged?)

- *What's really going on here?* (Because surface problems usually have deeper causes, and I couldn't fix what I didn't understand.)

- *Can this person be restored, or do I need to protect the people they're hurting?* (Because grace and accountability aren't opposites, they're two sides of the same coin.)

- *Does this feel right?* (Not politically convenient, not emotionally satisfying, but *right* in that gut-level way when you strip away all the noise.)

I didn't realize I was building a framework. I was just trying to survive. Trying to lead better than the people who'd led me. Trying to create an environment where people didn't wake up dreading Monday morning. It worked. Not perfectly, but consistently enough that I kept using it. The principles held under pressure. People trusted me. Teams performed. Culture formed. I thought I'd figured something out. That I'd built something through sheer force of experience and observation. That I was smarter than the bosses who'd failed me because I'd learned from their mistakes. I was wrong.

The Day Everything Changed

In May 2023, I found Christ. I'm not going to bore you with a conversion story full of spiritual clichés. But something shifted. Something I'd been sitting in a church ignoring for sixteen years, something I'd dismissed since I was a teenager, suddenly became the most real thing in my life. I started reading the Bible. Actually reading it, not just dismissing it as ancient mythology, and as I read, something strange started happening. Well, strange to me, but all part of God's plan.

I kept finding my framework. The humility I'd learned to practice?

> **Galatians 6:1**: *"If anyone is caught in any transgression, you who are spiritual should restore him in a spirit of gentleness. Keep watch on yourself, lest you too be tempted."*

The emphasis on understanding whole counsel before judging?

> **Proverbs 18:13**: *"If one
> gives an answer before he
> hears, it is his folly and
> shame."*

The balance between restoration and protection? **Galatians 6:2** says bear one another's burdens. But **Ezekiel 34:4** condemns leaders who fail to protect the vulnerable. Both are true. Both are necessary.

The moral intuition shaped by principle?

> **Romans 12:2** talks about
> being *"transformed by the
> renewal of your mind, that
> by testing you may discern
> what is the will of God."*

Every principle I thought I'd discovered on my own, every lesson I thought I'd learned through hard experience, every framework component I thought I'd built from scratch, it was already there. In a book written thousands of years ago. By people who'd never heard of tech companies or production databases or quarterly earnings calls. At first, I was annoyed. I'd spent sixteen years figuring this out, and it turns out someone had already written it down? Then something hit me, something that changed how I see everything:

I hadn't built this framework. I'd discovered it.

The principles weren't true because the Bible said them. They were in the Bible because they're true. They're descriptions of reality. Of how people actually work. How trust is actually built. How change actually happens. How justice and mercy actually intersect. When I'd been pursuing what was actually true, actually effective, actually right, even as an atheist with no interest in religion, I'd been stumbling toward the same truths Scripture had been describing all along.

By the grace of God, they aligned.

Not because I was trying to be Christian. But because God's truth is woven into reality itself. You can't escape it, even if you don't believe in it. When you pursue what's true, you're pursuing Him, whether you know it or not. I'd been functioning as a Christian without realizing it. Not in the saved-by-grace sense. Not in the theological sense. But in the practical sense: I'd been operating according to principles that align with how God designed reality to work. There's only one reality and God made it. The Bible describes it accurately. You can discover those truths whether you believe in the Bible or not, just by paying attention to what actually works when you test it under pressure.

The Humbling Realization

Here's what that realization did to me: it destroyed my pride and expanded my perspective at the same time. I'd thought I was smart. That I'd figured something out through experience and observation. That I'd built a framework from scratch.

But I hadn't built anything. I'd just been paying attention. And the principles I'd discovered, billions of people had discovered them before me, across millennia, across cultures, across every context imaginable. Not because we're all reading the same book, but because we're all living in the same reality.

And that reality was designed by Someone much smarter than me. With a much bigger plan than I could see. Who'd already described how things actually work in a book I'd spent forty years dismissing.

> **Proverbs 16:9** says, *"The heart of man plans his way, but the Lord establishes his steps."*

I'd been planning my way, building my framework, figuring out my principles. But God had been establishing my steps. Leading me toward truth even when I didn't believe in Him. Shaping me according to principles I didn't know came from Him. That's humbling and profound. It changes everything about how I see leadership, faith, and the intersection of the two.

Who This Book Is For

If you're a Christian leader, I wrote this for you.

Not to give you more religious jargon. Not to help you "witness at work" in some awkward, forced way. I wrote this to show you what integrated faith actually looks like. You don't have "Sunday you" and "Monday you." You're one person, and Biblical truth should shape how you see everything, not just "spiritual" things. Not by quoting Scripture in every meeting, but by letting Scripture shape your operating system, the lens through which you see people, problems, and pressure.

This book will show you a framework that works in the real world, under real pressure, with real consequences. Not theory. Not ideal scenarios. Actual decisions about production outages, harassment reports, billing mistakes, and everything else that makes leadership hard. You'll see how that framework is rooted in Scripture, not because I was trying to be religious, but because I was trying to be true and by the grace of God, they're the same thing.

I also wrote this for leaders who don't share my faith.

Maybe you're an atheist like I was. Maybe you're agnostic, skeptical, or just not interested in religion. You might be wondering why you should care about a book with "Christian" in the title. Here's why: because these principles work whether you believe in the Bible or not.

I built this framework while sitting in church chairs with my mind elsewhere, while living without active faith, while treating religion as irrelevant to my actual life. I developed and tested it for about seven years without any reference to Scripture and it worked. Not because I was secretly Christian. But because the principles are true, and truth works when you apply it, regardless of whether you acknowledge the source.

You don't have to pray to recognize that **humility** produces better decisions than arrogance. You don't have to go to church to see that understanding **whole counsel** leads to wiser outcomes. You don't have to believe in God to observe that **grace** often accomplishes more than punishment.

These aren't religious platitudes. They're battle-tested principles forged in crisis, refined through failure, proven under pressure.

They're available to anyone willing to pursue what's actually true instead of what's convenient. Test them. Adapt them. See if they hold up in your context. I think you'll find they do. Not because I'm asking you to take my faith, but because I'm inviting you to test principles that describe reality accurately.

If you're an atheist who finds that these principles work, maybe that tells you something. Maybe it means you're discovering the same truth I discovered: that reality has an Author, and His principles are woven into the fabric of existence itself, whether we acknowledge Him or not. Maybe you'll just find that ancient wisdom has something to say about your Tuesday meeting. Either way, the principles work.

What This Book Isn't

This isn't a book about how to evangelize your coworkers. I don't put Bible verses in my email signature. I don't lead prayer meetings in the break room. And I'm not going to tell you to do those things either. This isn't a book about being "nice." Biblical leadership isn't soft. Grace isn't weakness. Sometimes leadership requires firing people, correcting lies in front of clients, making decisions that cost you politically. You'll see all of that in this book.

This isn't a book of theory. Every principle, every story, every decision comes from actual situations with real consequences. Production outages at 2 AM. Harassment reports about employees from women who'd been watching me for months. A $350,000 billing mistake where I failed to follow my own framework and paid the price. This is the stuff that reveals whether your principles are real or just words you say when it's convenient.

This isn't a book about perfection. I've got three full chapters about the ways I still struggle, the rough edges I'm still working on, the gap between the leader I want to be and the leader I am when I'm frustrated and tired and done with people's excuses. This is a book about a framework that holds when feelings don't. About principles tested under pressure. About leadership that works because it's true, not because it's popular or easy.

It's a book about the stunning reality that an atheist can build a framework through trial and error that aligns with Biblical truth, because God's truth isn't confined to believers. It's woven into reality itself. Anyone pursuing what's true will eventually discover it.

The Framework

Over about seven years of building it without faith, then discovering it aligned with Scripture after my conversion, through crisis and consequence and countless decisions under pressure, this is the framework that emerged:

1. Humility: Who am I to judge? What am I missing?

Before you decide what to do about someone else, check your own capacity for the same failure. Have you ever done what they just did? Are you judging them more harshly than you'd want to be judged? What blind spots might you have?

2. Whole Counsel: What's the complete human and business impact?

Don't make decisions based on incomplete information. See the whole person, not just the failure. Understand the whole situation, not just the surface problem. What's really going on here?

3. Restoration or Protection: Can this be fixed, or does someone need defending?

When someone fails, can they be restored? If yes, invest in restoration. Grace builds loyalty and people grow, but if the pattern persists and people are being harmed, protection becomes necessary. Both matter. Discernment is knowing which the moment requires.

4. Moral Intuition: Does this feel right based on principles, not politics?

After considering humility, context, and whether restoration or protection is needed, ask: Does this align with what's true and good and just? Not "Will this make people happy?" Not "Is this expedient?" But does this feel right in your gut when you strip away the pressure and the politics?

That's the framework. Simple enough to remember under pressure. Deep enough to handle the complexity of real human situations. Flexible enough to apply across contexts, and grounded enough in truth that it holds when everything else is falling apart.

> An atheist built it. The Bible describes it. Both were pointing at the same reality.

What You'll Find in This Book

Part 1: The Education of Pain tells the story of the bad bosses who taught me what not to do. Each chapter is a failure mode I watched destroy trust, and the principle I built from the wreckage. This is where the framework came from, forged in crisis as an atheist with no interest in religion, just trying to lead better than the people who'd led me.

Part 2: The Framework in Action shows you the big decisions where this framework was tested under real pressure. The junior analyst who deleted production data and the pressure to fire her. The inappropriate employee who had to be removed after three chances.

The sales meeting where I had to correct lies in front of a client. The billing mistake where I failed to follow my own framework and it cost us everything. These aren't sanitized case studies. They're real decisions with real consequences.

Part 3: Building the Culture is about the small decisions that compound over time. How to hire for character. How to make collaborative decisions without losing leadership. How the daily behaviors no one notices become the reputation that allows people to trust you with what matters most. This is where principles become culture.

Part 4: The Rough Edges is the honest part most leadership books skip. When frustration wins and you're not the leader you want to be. When you struggle to receive feedback from people whose judgment you don't respect. When you realize you have favorites and you're not sure if it's wisdom or partiality. This is me admitting I'm still being shaped, still growing, still wrestling with the gap between principle and practice, although there is plenty of that sprinkled throughout.

Part 5: The Integrated Life brings it all together. What it means to stop compartmentalizing faith and work. How to be ready when people ask why you lead differently. Why the long view matters more than quarterly results. This is where the atheist framework and the Biblical foundation converge, where you see they were describing the same reality all along.

The Promise

If you read this book and apply these principles, here's what I can promise:

You'll have a framework that holds when the pressure's on. Not because it's perfect, but because it's rooted in what's actually true about people, trust, and leadership. Truth that works whether you acknowledge the source or not.

You'll make better decisions. Not popular decisions, not easy decisions, but decisions you can stand on when the outcome isn't what you hoped. Decisions based on principle, not convenience.

You'll build trust over time. Not immediately, maybe not even quickly, but consistency over time creates credibility and credibility becomes influence that lasts beyond your title, your position, your quarterly results.

If you're a Christian, you'll learn to integrate your faith in a way that's real, not forced. In a way that shows people the fruit of Biblical principles before you ever explain the roots. In a way that makes people curious about where your leadership comes from, because they've experienced something different and they want to understand why.

If you're not a Christian, you'll find principles that work. Test them. Push on them. See if they hold in your context, and maybe, just maybe, you'll start wondering why someone building a framework through trial and error, someone sitting in church physically but not mentally for sixteen years, someone with no interest in applying religion to work, kept stumbling toward the same truths a 3,000-year-old book already described.

Maybe that tells you something about reality and about truth. About the possibility that Someone actually designed this whole thing and left His fingerprints everywhere, even in the leadership principles someone discovers when they're just trying not to destroy trust the way their bad bosses did.

Or maybe you'll just find that the principles work. Either way, I'll take it.

The Journey Ahead

I was someone living without active faith, sitting in church chairs while my mind was elsewhere, building a framework through pain and pressure, thinking I was figuring it out on my own. I became a Christian in May 2023 and discovered I'd been discovering truth that was already there, already described, already proven across millennia and cultures.

By the grace of God, they aligned. Not because I was smart, but because He's already written His truth into reality itself. You can't escape it. You can only discover it or ignore it. This book is that discovery. The framework built in crisis. The Biblical foundation found later. The stunning realization that they were pointing at the same thing all along.

Whether you're a Christian trying to integrate your faith into your leadership, or a skeptic looking for principles that actually hold under pressure, this framework works. Not because I invented it, but because it's true.

Truth works. Every time. Whether you believe in the source or not. Let me show you how.

Part 1

Most people build their leadership philosophy from books, mentors, or MBA programs. I built mine from wreckage.

Four bad bosses over eighteen years taught me more about leadership than any classroom could have. Not because they showed me the right way, but because they showed me every wrong way possible. They taught me what destroys trust, what breeds resentment, what drives good people away, and what makes leadership toxic instead of transformative.

The email hacker who treated people like threats to be monitored. The hotheaded genius whose ego made him unteachable. The absentee king who demanded presence from everyone but himself. The trust breaker who promised confidentiality and delivered betrayal fifteen minutes later. Each one created damage I had to watch unfold. Each one taught me exactly what I swore never to become.

This section isn't about holding grudges. It's about learning from negative examples. Sometimes the best teacher is the one who shows you precisely what happens when you get it wrong. If you pay attention to the wreckage, you start to see patterns. Principles that hold. Questions that matter. A framework emerging from the pain.

By the end of these chapters, you'll see how four different failure modes pointed toward the same truth, how watching leadership destroy teams taught me what actually builds them, and how an atheist with no interest in religion stumbled toward Biblical principles just by trying not to inflict the same damage on others.

Pain is an excellent teacher. If you let it be.

Chapter One

The Email Hacker

Most people learn leadership from mentors who show them the right way. I learned it from bosses who showed me every wrong way possible. That's not the story I wanted. I didn't set out to build a leadership philosophy through pain. I didn't choose the education of failure, betrayal, and watching authority figures destroy everything they touched. But that's the education I got, and looking back, I'm not sure I'd trade it.

Good leaders can teach you what to do. Bad leaders teach you why it matters. Good leaders give you principles to follow. Bad leaders show you the consequences when those principles are violated. Good leaders inspire. Bad leaders create urgency. When you watch a leader destroy trust, you don't just learn that trust is important. You feel the weight of broken relationships. You see good people quit. You experience the culture of fear that replaces psychological safety. You carry the damage, and you swear you'll never inflict that on someone else.

Over eighteen years in my career, I've worked for and alongside every kind of bad boss imaginable. The micromanager who couldn't trust anyone. The egomaniac who thought vocal volume equaled value. The absent leader who demanded presence from everyone else.

The trust-breaker who promised confidentiality and delivered betrayal. Each one taught me something I couldn't have learned any other way.

This isn't a chapter about holding grudges or settling scores. These leaders probably never intended to become cautionary tales. Most of them thought they were doing a good job. Some might have even believed they were helping me. Intention doesn't change impact, and the impact they had on me, on my teams, and on how I understand leadership is foundational to everything I've built since.

Before I show you the framework that works, let me show you the wreckage that taught me why it had to work. Before I tell you what I do now, let me show you what I learned never to do. Before you trust my principles, let me prove them through the negative examples that shaped them. Sometimes the best teacher is the one who shows you exactly what happens when you get it wrong.

The Violation

I noticed something was off when emails I hadn't opened were showing as read. At first, I thought it was a glitch. Maybe my phone had synced weird. Maybe the email client had a bug. Then I checked the account access logs. There it was. A login from Firefox. I only used Firefox for debugging web applications, never for personal email. The IP address wasn't from my home network or my phone. It was from the office where I worked.

Someone had been in my personal email. Not just once. Multiple times. Different days, different times. Someone had systematically gone through my inbox, reading correspondence that had nothing to do with work. I knew exactly who it was. My boss had broken into my personal email because he suspected I was looking for a new job, and he was right. I was actively job hunting. Not because I didn't like the work or lacked opportunity. Because the environment he'd created was suffocating, and I was looking for a way out.

When he confirmed what he suspected, he didn't have the decency to keep quiet about his invasion of privacy. He confronted me. Accused me. Threatened to fire me for the audacity of looking elsewhere. The message was clear: You belong to me. Your loyalty isn't something I earn. It's something I demand and enforce.

The Anger

I've felt a lot of emotions in my career. Frustration when projects fail. Disappointment when people let me down. Stress when deadlines loom. But what I felt in that moment was different. It was white-hot anger mixed with absolute disgust.

Not just because he'd violated my privacy, though that was bad enough, but because his actions confirmed everything I'd suspected about his leadership. He didn't trust anyone. He saw people as threats to be monitored, not team members to be developed. His insecurity manifested as authoritarian control, and anyone who didn't submit completely became an enemy.

Here's the twisted irony: He'd created the exact environment that drove me to look for other jobs. His paranoia, his control, his inability to trust had made working there unbearable, and then he surveilled me for having the audacity to respond rationally to the culture he'd built. I wasn't looking for a job because I was disloyal. I was looking because he'd made it impossible to stay.

The Broader Surveillance State

Here's what I realized later: The email hacking wasn't an isolated incident. It was just the most egregious example of a leadership philosophy built on surveillance. He was always watching. Standing behind people's desks, looking over their shoulders at their screens. Walking the floor to see who was "really working" and who was taking breaks. Double-checking work that had already been completed, not to ensure quality, but to catch mistakes he could use as evidence of incompetence. Monitoring when people arrived and left, not because hours mattered for the work, but because presence could be measured and controlled. Every interaction felt like an audit. Every conversation felt recorded. Every decision felt scrutinized for hidden motives.

You don't need to hack someone's email to create a surveillance state. You can do it with your physical presence, your management style, your inability to delegate without hovering. You can build it through policies that assume guilt until proven innocent, through systems that track every minute of the day, through cultures where people feel watched instead of trusted. The email hacking was just the digital version of what he'd been doing all along: treating people like threats to be monitored instead of team members to be trusted.

What I Learned

That boss taught me more about leadership than he ever intended. Not through his example, but through the wreckage he left behind. **You can't control people into loyalty.** He thought surveillance would keep people in line. All it did was drive away anyone with options. The people who stayed weren't loyal. They were trapped, and the moment they found an escape route, they took it.

Trust destroyed can't be rebuilt through force. Once I knew he'd invaded my privacy, every interaction was poisoned. I didn't trust anything he said. I assumed every conversation was recorded, every email monitored, every move scrutinized. You can't build a relationship on surveillance. You just create prisoners looking for parole.

Insecurity in leaders destroys everyone around them. His behavior wasn't about me. It was about him. He was so insecure in his own leadership that he couldn't imagine people staying by choice. So he tried to keep them through control, and in doing so, he guaranteed they'd leave the moment they could. **Fear-based leadership drives away good people.** The people who could leave, did. The ones who stayed were either unable to find other options or willing to tolerate abuse. That's not a team. That's a hostage situation with paychecks.

How I Lead Differently

I carry that experience with me every day. Not as a wound, but as a warning. A reminder of what leadership becomes when trust is replaced by control. **I don't demand loyalty. I try to earn it.** People stay on my teams because they want to, not because they're trapped. If someone's looking for other opportunities, that's data. Either I've failed to create an environment worth staying in, or they've found something better aligned with their goals. Both are legitimate. Neither require surveillance to discover.

I build cultures of psychological safety, not surveillance. People should feel free to speak truth, to fail, to disagree, to grow. The moment they feel watched and judged, they start performing instead of producing. They optimize for looking good instead of being honest and you lose the very thing that makes teams functional: trust.

I don't stand over people's shoulders checking their work. I don't double-check completed tasks looking for mistakes to critique. I don't monitor arrival and departure times as if hours worked equals value created. I don't create policies that assume people will take advantage unless constantly watched.

When I delegate, I actually delegate. I trust people to do their jobs. If that trust turns out to be misplaced, we have a conversation about expectations and performance but I start from trust, not suspicion. **I lead from security, not insecurity.** Good people don't need to be monitored. They need to be supported. If I can't trust someone to do their job without surveillance, I shouldn't have hired them and if I did hire them and they're not performing, that's a conversation about expectations and fit, not an excuse for creating a culture of monitoring.

The question isn't "How do I make sure people are working?" The question is "Have I hired people I can trust, given them clear expectations, and created an environment where they can succeed?" If the answer is yes, surveillance is insulting. If the answer is no, surveillance won't fix it.

I give people freedom instead of chains. Scripture consistently models leadership through trust and empowerment, not control and surveillance. In Genesis 1-2, God entrusts humans with dominion over creation, giving them responsibility and freedom within boundaries. Even knowing they could fail, God doesn't micromanage or surveil, He trusts them with stewardship.

Jesus modeled the same pattern. In John 15:15, He says, "No longer do I call you servants... but I have called you friends." He entrusted His disciples with the entire mission (Matthew 28:18-20), sent them out with authority (Luke 10), and didn't hover over them after He ascended. That's trust-based leadership.

In Matthew 25, Jesus tells the parable of the talents, where the master entrusts servants with significant resources and leaves them to steward independently. The servants who operated in freedom thrived. The one who operated in fear buried his talent and was condemned for it. Fear-based leadership produces buried-talent employees. Control creates compliance. Freedom creates ownership.

The Biblical Foundation

Scripture is consistently clear about how authority should be exercised:

> **1 Peter 5:2-3** tells leaders to "shepherd the flock of God that is among you, exercising oversight, not under compulsion, but willingly, as God would have you; not for shameful gain, but eagerly; not domineering over those in your charge, but being examples to the flock."

Notice the contrast: shepherding vs. domineering. Willing oversight vs. compulsion. Example vs. control. My email-hacking boss wasn't shepherding, he was domineering. And in doing so, he scattered the flock.

> **Ephesians 6:9** commands those in authority: "Masters, do the same to them, and stop your threatening, knowing that he who is both their Master and yours is in heaven, and that there is no partiality with him."

Leaders who lead through threat and surveillance forget they themselves answer to a Master who treats them with dignity and trust.

> **Matthew 20:25-28** shows Jesus explicitly contrast-
> ing worldly leadership with His model: "You know
> that the rulers of the Gentiles lord it over them, and
> their great ones exercise authority over them. It shall
> not be so among you... whoever would be great among
> you must be your servant."

"Lord it over" is exactly what surveillance-based leadership does. It dominates, controls, and treats people as subjects to be managed rather than co-laborers to be trusted.

There's a difference between Biblical accountability and sinful surveillance:

- **Biblical accountability** is shepherding, knowing your people, caring for their growth, holding them responsible for outcomes

- **Sinful surveillance** is domineering, treating people as threats, monitoring out of insecurity, controlling out of fear

My email-hacking boss wasn't practicing Biblical oversight. He was practicing sinful control and the fruit proved it: good people fled, trust evaporated, and fear replaced flourishing.

The Secular Case

You don't need to believe the Bible to understand why surveil-lance-based leadership fails. The business case is overwhelming:

- **High performers leave.** People with options don't tolerate being treated like criminals. They take their skills, their experience, and their potential somewhere they're trusted. You're

left with people who can't leave, not people who choose to
stay.

- **Innovation dies.** Psychological safety is the foundation of
  creativity. When people are being monitored, they optimize
  for not making mistakes, not for trying new things. You get
  compliance, not innovation. Safety, not breakthroughs.

- **Trust becomes impossible.** Every relationship in the organization gets poisoned by the culture of surveillance. People
  don't collaborate honestly. They cover their tracks. They
  play politics. They protect themselves instead of advancing
  the mission.

You become the thing you fear. Leaders who don't trust their
people create self-fulfilling prophecies. People respond to being treated like threats by becoming less trustworthy. Not because they're bad
people, but because survival in that environment requires secrecy and
self-protection.

My Rough Edges

I wish I could tell you I learned this lesson so well that I never struggle
with it. But that would be dishonest. **I struggle to trust after betrayal.** When someone breaks my trust, my instinct is to never extend
it again. I have to consciously fight against that impulse, to separate
the person who betrayed me from the next person who needs trust to
function.

My default is skepticism with some people. Not everyone. But
people who've demonstrated poor judgment, who've burned trust
before, who've shown patterns I've learned to recognize. I have to

intentionally choose trust instead of suspicion. It doesn't come naturally.

Under pressure, I'm tempted to tighten control. When stress is high, when deadlines are crushing, when stakes are massive, my instinct is to micromanage. To check everything. To tighten my grip instead of trusting the team I've built. I have to recognize that impulse for what it is: my own insecurity, not a legitimate response to the situation.

I know what surveillance-based leadership produces. I've lived under it. I've seen the wreckage and yet, the temptation to control instead of trust still surfaces in me. Usually when I'm afraid. Usually when I feel vulnerable. Usually when my own insecurity starts driving my decisions. That's when I remember that boss and I remember what his fear built and I choose differently.

The Choice Every Leader Makes

You can't build a team on surveillance. You can only build a prison. You can't create loyalty through control. You can only manufacture compliance until people find the exit. You can't lead from fear and expect people to follow with courage.

My email-hacking boss taught me that the hard way. He built an empire of fear and lost everyone worth keeping. He demanded loyalty and got performance. He tried to control outcomes and lost the very thing that makes organizations work: people who choose to give their best because they're trusted to do so. I learned from his failure. Not because he intended to teach me, but because pain is an excellent educator.

The question every leader faces:

- Will you lead from security or insecurity?

- Will you trust or surveil?

- Will you create cultures of freedom or cultures of fear?

Your people already know the answer. It shows up in a thousand small decisions. Whether you trust them to work remotely or demand they're in the office where you can see them. Whether you give autonomy or require approval for every decision. Whether you assume good intent or suspect malice.

They know and they're making their own decisions based on what they see. Choose trust. Even when it's scary. Even when you've been burned. Even when control feels safer. The alternative isn't leadership. It's just fear dressed up in authority.

Next: Chapter 2 will explore what I learned from the boss who thought volume equaled value, ego equaled leadership, and shouting was the same as being right. Spoiler: It wasn't

Chapter Two

The Hotheaded Stud

I f the email-hacking boss taught me that control destroys trust, the hotheaded boss taught me that volume doesn't equal value.

The Performance

He drove a lifted truck. Not just any truck, but the kind that announces your presence three blocks before you arrive. Chrome everywhere. Oversized tires. The vehicular equivalent of shouting "Look at me!" That truck was the perfect metaphor for his leadership style: loud, flashy, impossible to ignore, and desperate for attention.

He yelled. Constantly. At everyone. About everything. It wasn't passionate intensity or righteous anger. It was his default communication mode. If you could hear him from across the office, which you always could, he was probably telling someone how brilliant his latest idea was or explaining why they were failing to grasp his genius.

He thought he was God's gift to the world. The smartest person in every room. The only one who really understood the business, the technology, the customers, the future. Everyone else was just lucky to be in his presence. His ideas? Terrible. Consistently, predictably, almost impressively terrible. But you couldn't tell him that. Because to challenge his ideas was to challenge his identity. And that's when the yelling got louder.

The Encryption Disaster

Early in my career, he decided we needed better security for our application. Fair enough. Data security matters. But instead of using established encryption libraries that had been tested, vetted, and proven by people who actually understood cryptography, he decided to roll his own encryption scheme. He was absolutely convinced it was brilliant. Cutting edge. Revolutionary. He explained it to the team with the confidence of someone who'd just solved a problem that had stumped the entire security industry.

Even with my limited experience at the time, I could see the problems. He'd created an encryption algorithm, sure. But he stored the encryption key right alongside the encrypted data. Like locking your front door and leaving the key under the doormat. Except worse, because he'd also created a publicly accessible web form at aaaaaaa.aspx where anyone could paste an encrypted value and get the unencrypted value back.

Let me be clear: He built a public decryption tool. Available to anyone with internet access. For the encryption scheme protecting our data. This wasn't just bad. This was a security professional's nightmare. It was the equivalent of installing a bank vault with a neon sign saying "Here's how to open it!" He was certain it was brilliant, and when I tried, carefully, to raise concerns about the approach, the yelling started.

The Public Humiliation

I don't remember the exact words. What I remember is the volume. The entire office could hear him tearing into me for "not understanding security" and "questioning his expertise." He didn't pull me aside. He didn't schedule a meeting. He just started yelling, right there in the open office, about how I didn't know what I was talking about, how his solution was sophisticated and I just couldn't grasp it, how I should be grateful to learn from someone with his experience.

I stood there, face burning, watching coworkers pretend to focus on their screens while my competence was being publicly demolished by someone who'd just created the digital equivalent of a screen door on a submarine. The worst part wasn't the yelling. It was knowing he was completely, objectively wrong, and there was no way to make him see it. His ego had completely blinded him to reality. And anyone who tried to help him see reality became an enemy.

Eventually, we quietly implemented actual encryption libraries, but not before his "solution" had been in production for months, exposing customer data in ways that still make me cringe.

What I Learned

Volume doesn't equal competence. The loudest voice in the room is often compensating for the weakest argument. People who actually know what they're talking about don't need to yell. They can explain, discuss, and even admit uncertainty. The yelling was his tell. It meant he was protecting ego, not pursuing truth.

Ego blinds you to your own limitations. He couldn't see how bad his ideas were because his identity was wrapped up in being the smartest person around. Admitting he was wrong about encryption would mean admitting he wasn't the genius he'd built his self-image around. So instead, he doubled down on objectively terrible ideas and attacked anyone who questioned them.

External flashiness often masks internal insecurity. The truck, the yelling, the need to dominate every conversation, all of it screamed insecurity. Secure people don't need to prove themselves constantly. They're comfortable with what they don't know. They can admit mistakes. They don't need to be the hero of every story.

Leaders who can't be wrong can't learn. Every terrible idea he insisted on was a missed opportunity to grow. Every person he shouted down was someone who might have taught him something. But learning requires humility. And humility requires admitting you might not have all the answers. He'd rather be loudly wrong than quietly teachable.

Teams can't function when ego trumps truth. The best idea should win. Not the loudest idea. Not the idea from the highest-ranking person. Not the idea that makes someone feel smart. The best idea, regardless of whose mouth it comes from. When ego determines which ideas get implemented, the team optimizes for making the boss feel good instead of actually solving problems.

How I Lead Differently

I carry scars from that environment. But I also carry lessons that shape how I lead every day. **I say "I'm rarely the smartest in the room" and I mean it.** That's not false humility. That's reality. I've hired people smarter than me in their domains because that's how you build great teams. My job isn't to have all the answers. It's to create environments where the best answers emerge, regardless of who has them.

I build cultures where the best idea wins. Not the loudest. Not mine because I'm the CTO. The best idea, tested against reality, proven through discussion, refined through collaboration. That means I have to be willing to be wrong. Publicly. Regularly. And model that being wrong isn't a character flaw, it's a learning opportunity.

I filter for ego in hiring. I have an interview process specifically designed to test whether candidates can admit they're wrong and accept better ideas from others. I'd rather have a thousand humble people who can learn than one brilliant person who thinks they know everything. Ego is poison in teams. It spreads, it corrupts, and it drives away good people who don't want to spend their lives managing someone's fragile self-image.

I never yell. Not because I never get frustrated. I do. But because yelling is about power, not leadership. It's about making someone feel small so you can feel big. It's about shutting down discussion instead of opening it up. And it creates cultures where people are afraid to speak truth.

I check my own ego regularly. Because here's the thing I learned from watching him: ego is sneaky. It doesn't announce itself. It doesn't show up waving flags. It shows up in subtle ways. In the frustration when someone doesn't immediately grasp what I'm explaining. In the impatience when people think slower than I do. In the snap judgment that someone just doesn't get it.

I still struggle with all of those. I feel the frustration rise when someone makes what seems like an obviously bad decision. I get impatient when people need more time to process. Certain personality types still trigger something in me that wants to dismiss them. When that happens, I don't yell. I get quiet. My face shows everything. That's just a different form of the same ego problem. It's saying "I'm frustrated that you're not as competent as me" without using words. I'm still working on that. Every day.

The Biblical Foundation

Scripture has a lot to say about pride, humility, and the danger of unteachable leaders:

> **Proverbs 16:18** "Pride goes before destruction, and a haughty spirit before a fall."

I watched that play out in real time. His pride in his encryption brilliance led directly to security disasters. His haughty spirit in dismissing input led to bad decisions that hurt the company. The verse isn't just a moral warning, it's a description of how God designed reality to work. Pride is both sinful (an offense against God who alone deserves preeminence) and destructive (violating the created order produces natural consequences). When leaders refuse to acknowledge their limitations, they're not just being impractical, they're usurping God's position and treating themselves as the ultimate authority. Reality doesn't tolerate that for long.

> **Proverbs 29:11** "A fool gives full vent to his spirit, but a wise man quietly holds it back."

The yelling wasn't strength. It was lack of self-control. It was emotional incontinence masquerading as passion. Wise leaders don't need to dominate every conversation with volume.

James 1:19 "Let every person be quick to hear, slow to speak, slow to anger."

Quick to hear means actually listening to input, especially input that challenges your assumptions. Slow to speak means not dominating conversations with your own ideas. Slow to anger means not yelling at people who question you. He did the exact opposite of all three.

Proverbs 12:15 "The way of a fool is right in his own eyes, but a wise man listens to advice."

His way was always right in his own eyes. The encryption scheme, the business decisions, the people management, all of it, and because he couldn't listen to advice, he stayed foolish.

Proverbs 26:12 "Do you see a man who is wise in his own eyes? There is more hope for a fool than for him."

Not much hope for a fool. But less hope for someone who thinks they're wise. Because fools can learn. But people convinced of their own wisdom have closed the door to growth.

The Secular Case

You don't need Scripture to understand why ego-driven leadership fails:

- **Innovation dies.** When the boss's ego determines which ideas move forward, you don't get the best solutions. You get the solutions that make the boss feel smart. Good ideas from junior people get dismissed. Challenges to bad ideas get punished. The team learns to stop contributing.

- **Good people leave.** High performers don't stick around to manage someone else's ego. They go somewhere their ideas are valued and their expertise is trusted. You're left with people who either can't leave or have learned to nod along with whatever the boss says. Neither group builds great companies.

- **Bad decisions compound.** When you can't admit you're wrong, you can't course-correct. That encryption disaster should have been caught immediately. But ego prevented the correction. So the bad decision stayed in place, creating more problems, requiring more cover-ups, digging the hole deeper. One bad decision, protected by ego, becomes ten bad decisions.

- **Trust evaporates.** When people watch the boss yell at anyone who challenges them, two things happen: They stop challenging, and they stop trusting. They learn the game is about ego management, not problem solving. And once that becomes the game, you've lost everything that makes organizations work.

- **Culture becomes toxic.** Ego is contagious. When the leader models "I'm always right and anyone who questions me is an idiot," that becomes the culture. Everyone starts protecting their ego. Politics replace collaboration. Blame replaces learning. And the whole organization optimizes for looking good instead of being good.

My Rough Edges

I wish I could tell you I'm completely free from the ego problems I saw in him, but I'm not. I still get frustrated with incompetence. When someone makes a decision that seems obviously wrong, I feel that surge of impatience. Part of my brain goes "How did you not see that?" And I have to consciously fight against dismissing them.

I struggle with people who think slowly. My processing speed is fast. I see patterns quickly, make connections rapidly, jump to conclusions that usually turn out right. And when someone needs more time to work through something I've already figured out, I get impatient. That's ego talking. That's me valuing my processing speed over their thorough analysis.

Certain personality types trigger me. People who are overly confident without basis. People who talk a lot but say little. People who've demonstrated poor judgment repeatedly. I'm tempted to write them off, to stop listening when they talk, to dismiss their input before I've even heard it. That's ego. That's me deciding I know better without actually engaging with what they're saying.

I don't yell, but I get quiet. And my face shows everything. So instead of making people feel small with volume, I make them feel small with silence and obvious frustration. Different delivery, same ego problem. Same message: "I'm disappointed you're not better."

I'm working on all of this. Some days are better than others. The difference between me and that hotheaded boss isn't that I've conquered ego. It's that I'm aware it's a problem. I'm willing to admit it. I'm actively fighting against it. And I'm trying to build systems and cultures that work even when my ego shows up.

Because here's what I learned from watching him: Ego doesn't just destroy your leadership. It destroys your ability to see that it's destroying your leadership. The yelling, the dismissiveness, the inability to hear input, all of it seemed justified to him. He thought he was being strong. He thought he was being decisive. He thought he was being a leader. He was wrong and the wreckage he left behind proved it.

The Choice Every Leader Makes

You can lead from ego or you can lead from humility. You can't do both.

- Ego says: I need to be the smartest person in the room. I need to have all the answers. I need to prove my worth by being right. Anyone who challenges me is a threat.

- Humility says: I need to find the smartest people and create space for them. I need to ask better questions. I prove my worth by getting to the truth, not by being right. Anyone who challenges me might be helping.

Your team knows which one you've chosen. They hear it in how you respond to being questioned. They see it in whose ideas get implemented. They feel it in whether the culture optimizes for truth or for making you feel good. Choose humility. Even when ego feels safer. Even when being wrong feels like failure. Even when you really do think you're right. The loudest person in the room is rarely the most competent and the leader who can't be wrong can't be trusted.

Next: Chapter 3 will explore the boss who demanded everyone be present while he led from a distance. Because "do as I say, not as I do" destroys credibility faster than any other leadership failure.

Chapter Three

The Absentee King

I f the email hacker taught me that control destroys trust, and the hotheaded boss taught me that volume doesn't equal value, the absentee leader taught me that you can't lead from a distance while demanding presence from everyone else.

The Double Standard

He worked from home. Not occasionally. Not when the weather was bad or he had a plumber coming. Constantly. His default location was his home office, not the actual office where the team worked.

But here's the twist: Everyone else had to be on-site. Every day. No exceptions. No flexibility. No working from home when you needed focus time or had a family obligation. The office was where work happened, and if you weren't there, you weren't working. Except him, because apparently, different rules applied when you were in charge.

When anyone questioned this arrangement, the answer was always the same: "It's part of my benefits package." As if "benefits" meant "exemption from the standards I impose on everyone else." The message was clear: Leadership means getting privileges, not setting examples.

The Production Outage

The hypocrisy hit hardest during a production outage. The system went down hard. Customers couldn't access the application. The team was scrambling to diagnose the problem, fix the code, and get services restored. These are the moments when you need leadership. When decisions have to be made fast, when resources need to be allocated, when someone needs to take responsibility.

He was working from home. We tried calling. Got voicemail. Tried again. Left messages. Sent emails. The system was down, users were furious, and the person who was supposed to be leading us was unavailable because he'd prioritized his comfort over his team's needs. Eventually, we made the decisions ourselves. Fixed the problem. Got the system back up. Did the postmortem. The team handled it because the team had to, but the resentment? That didn't get fixed. That stayed and festered.

When you demand presence from your team while remaining absent yourself, you're saying their time matters less than yours. Their convenience is negotiable. Their families can wait. But yours can't. You're saying leadership is about privilege, not responsibility.

The Resentment Culture

People talked about it openly. Not quietly in corners, but out loud. The unfairness was so obvious that pretending it wasn't happening felt ridiculous.

- "He's probably at home in his pajamas while we're all stuck here."

- "Must be nice to have benefits that exempt you from reality."

- "Why are we required to be here when he never is?"

- Some even started working from home without permission because "who is going to know?"

The resentment wasn't just about the physical absence. It was about the principle. The "do as I say, not as I do" philosophy that permeated everything he did. The rules applied to everyone but him. The standards were for the peasants, not the king, and when people resent their leader, they don't give discretionary effort. They don't go above and beyond. They don't solve problems proactively. They show up, do exactly what's required, and leave. Compliance theater. Present in body, absent in engagement.

That's what his absent leadership created. A team that was technically there but emotionally checked out. Because if he didn't think presence mattered enough to show up himself, why should they think it mattered enough to actually engage?

What I Learned

Double standards destroy credibility instantly. You can't ask people to do what you're unwilling to do yourself. The moment people see that rules apply to them but not to you, you've lost them. Not eventually. Immediately. Trust evaporates, resentment fills the gap, and everything you try to lead after that happens through a lens of "easy for you to say."

This extends far beyond physical presence. It's about every hard thing you ask of your team. The late nights when production breaks. The difficult tasks nobody wants. The uncomfortable conversations. The grunt work that has to get done. If you're unwilling to do those things yourself, you have no business asking others to do them.

Leadership is presence. You can't lead from a distance and expect people to follow with commitment. Yes, you can issue directives. You can send emails. You can hold video calls but leadership isn't just communication. It's being in the trenches with your team. Feeling what they feel. Experiencing what they experience. Showing that you're not above the work, you're in it with them.

Presence means being there when the system crashes at 2am. It means taking on the tasks that are tedious or difficult. It means doing the work you're asking others to do, not exempting yourself because of your title. "Do as I say, not as I do" breeds resentment faster than almost anything else.

People can handle hard things. They can handle long hours, difficult problems, and challenging environments. What they can't handle is doing all of that while watching their leader opt out. The unfairness isn't just frustrating. It's fundamentally demoralizing.

I've watched leaders ask their teams to work weekends while they disconnect. I've seen leaders delegate the hardest problems while keeping the interesting work for themselves. I've heard leaders talk about sacrifice while protecting their own comfort. Every single time, it destroys morale.

You can't demand what you don't model. If you want people to be present, be present. If you want people to work hard, work hard. If you want people to sacrifice, sacrifice. Not because leadership is about suffering for no reason, but because people follow what you do, not what you say. Your behavior sets the standard. Everything else is just noise.

If you need someone to work overnight to fix a critical issue, you better be willing to work overnight too. If you need someone to take on the tedious task, you better be willing to take on tedious tasks yourself. If you expect responsiveness, you better be responsive. The standard you hold for yourself is the standard your team will internalize.

How I Lead Differently

I learned that leadership isn't about the perks you get to claim. It's about the example you're willing to set. I give people the freedom I want for myself. I believe in trust-based work environments. If someone can do their job effectively from home, I don't require them to be in the office just so I can see them. Judge by results, not by presence. Focus on outcomes, not on monitoring chairs.

Here's the key: I extend that same freedom to myself and to everyone on the team. If remote work makes sense for them, it makes sense for me. If I expect them to be somewhere, I'm there too. The standard is the same regardless of your title. I'm willing to work the hours I ask of my team. If the system crashes at 2am and we need to fix it, I'm there. Not just available by phone, but actually working alongside the team to solve the problem. If I ask someone to work a weekend to hit a deadline, I'm working that weekend too. I don't get to exempt myself from the hard hours because I'm in charge.

I take on the hardest tasks willingly. Not always, because part of my job is developing others by giving them challenging work. But when there's a task nobody wants, when there's a problem that's genuinely difficult, when there's work that's tedious but necessary, I don't automatically delegate it. I take my share of the grunt work, the difficult conversations, the problems without clear solutions. This has the added benefit of keeping my skills sharp.

If I'm not willing to do the hard things, why should anyone else be? I model what I expect. If I expect responsiveness during a crisis, I'm responsive during a crisis. If I expect people to be available when things break, I'm available when things break. If I expect people to show up for the hard conversations, I show up for the hard conversations. Not because I'm noble, because that's what leadership requires. You lead from the front, not from the rear issuing commands.

I'm present in the trenches. When the team is working through something difficult, I'm there. Not micromanaging. Not hovering. But present. Available. In it with them. Presence communicates value. It says "This matters enough that I'm here too." It says "You're not doing this alone." It says "The standard I'm asking of you is the standard I hold for myself."

I check my privilege regularly. Here's what I learned from watching him: Privilege is sneaky. It doesn't announce itself as unfairness. It justifies itself as earned benefits, reasonable accommodations, or just the way things work when you're in charge. "I've earned the right to work from home." "My time is more valuable, so I need to protect it." "I have strategic work that requires focus, so I can't be interrupted." All of those sound reasonable in isolation but when the result is a double standard, when the outcome is "different rules for me than for you," you've crossed from reasonable accommodation into privilege that destroys trust.

The Biblical Foundation

Scripture is consistently clear about leadership through example, not just through authority:

> **1 Corinthians 11:1** is Paul's bold claim: "Be imitators of me, as I am of Christ." Notice he doesn't say "Do what I tell you." He says "Imitate me." Follow my example. Look at how I live and do that. That only works if your life is worth imitating. If you're demanding things you don't model, that invitation becomes laughable.

> **John 1:14** tells us Jesus "became flesh and dwelt among us." The word "dwelt" literally means "pitched his tent." Jesus didn't lead from heaven, issuing commands remotely. He came down, lived among the people, experienced what they experienced. He led through presence, not just through pronouncements.

> **Philippians 2:5-7** describes Jesus' leadership: "Have this mind among yourselves, which is yours in Christ Jesus, who, though he was in the form of God, did not count equality with God a thing to be grasped, but emptied himself, by taking the form of a servant."

Jesus had every privilege. He gave them up to serve. He didn't leverage his position for comfort. He leveraged it for service. My absentee boss did the opposite. He leveraged his position for comfort. He claimed privilege while demanding sacrifice. He led from distance while requiring presence. That's the exact opposite of Christ's model.

> **1 Peter 5:3** tells leaders "not [to be] domineering over those in your charge, but being examples to the flock."

Examples. Not just authorities. Not just people who issue instructions. Examples whose lives demonstrate what they're asking others to do. When you demand presence while remaining absent, you're not being an example. You're being a domineering authority and people comply out of fear or obligation, not out of genuine followership.

The Secular Case

You don't need Scripture to see why absent leadership fails:

- **Resentment kills discretionary effort.** People do what's required and nothing more. They optimize for meeting the minimum standard, not for excellence. They don't proactively solve problems or go the extra mile. Why would they? The leader clearly doesn't value them enough to show up, so they return the favor.

- **Good people leave.** High performers don't stick around to be treated as second-class. They go somewhere their leaders model the standards they expect. They find environments where fairness actually matters. You're left with people who either can't leave or have learned to accept double standards as normal.

- **Culture becomes toxic.** When leadership operates by different rules, everyone starts looking for their own exceptions. "If he gets to work from home, I should get to come in late." "If his time is more valuable, mine must be too." The double standard doesn't stay contained. It spreads, and suddenly everyone's negotiating for their own special treatment.

- **Crisis response fails.** When things break, leadership matters most and if your leader isn't there when things break, the team learns they can't count on you. They learn to work around you instead of with you. You become irrelevant to the actual work, just an obstacle to route around.

- **Trust evaporates.** Once people see you claiming privileges you deny them, every other thing you say gets filtered through that lens. "Easy for you to say" becomes the internal response to every directive and once that's the default response, you've lost the ability to lead effectively.

My Rough Edges

I wish I could tell you I always get this right. But I don't. **I still value my own time more than I should.** When someone wants to meet and it's inconvenient for my schedule, my first instinct is to protect my time. To suggest they figure it out without me. To prioritize my focus over their need. I have to consciously push against that instinct and ask: Am I treating my time as more valuable than theirs? Is this a double standard?

When the system breaks at 2am, part of me wants to delegate it entirely. "Let the on-call person handle it." Sometimes that's appropriate. But sometimes I use delegation as an excuse to avoid the inconvenience I'm asking others to bear. **I'm tempted to delegate the hardest work.** Not because it's good for someone else's development, but because I don't want to do it. The tedious tasks. The difficult conversations. The problems that will take hours of grinding through details. My instinct is often to find someone else to handle it. I have to check myself: Am I delegating for their growth, or am I avoiding discomfort?

I still want the perks of leadership without all the costs. Leadership comes with both. You get more influence, more authority, more ability to shape direction but you also get more responsibility, more availability requirements, more obligation to model what you expect. I like the perks. I'm less enthusiastic about the costs and I have to regularly check that I'm not claiming one while avoiding the other.

I still sometimes justify distance as "strategic thinking." "I need to be out of the office to think about big picture stuff." Which can be true but it can also be an excuse to avoid the messiness of being present with the team. "Strategic" can become code for "comfortable distance from the actual work." I have to be honest about whether I'm actually doing strategic work or just enjoying the privilege of absence.

The Choice Every Leader Makes

You can lead from privilege or you can lead from example. You can't do both.

- **Privilege says:** I've earned different rules. My position comes with benefits. I get to opt out of the standards I impose on others.

- **Example says:** The standards I expect from others, I hold
  for myself first. My position comes with responsibility, not
  exemption. I lead by going first, not by staying back.

Your team already knows which one you've chosen. They see it in
whether you show up when things are hard. They feel it in whether
the rules apply equally. They experience it in whether your presence
matches your expectations and they make their own choices based on
what they see.

If you lead from privilege, they'll comply. They'll show up because
they have to. They'll do the minimum required. They'll resent you
quietly or openly depending on the culture and they'll leave the moment they can. If you lead from example, they'll follow. Not because
they have to, but because they want to. They'll give discretionary
effort. They'll solve problems proactively. They'll trust that when you
ask for something hard, you're willing to do hard things too.

The absentee king taught me that lesson through negative example.
He claimed privilege while demanding sacrifice. He led from comfort
while requiring presence. He issued commands from a distance while
expecting commitment up close. He lost everyone worth keeping.
Don't be that leader. Be present. Model what you expect. Hold yourself to the same standards you hold others. Lead from the trenches,
not from the tower. Leadership isn't about the benefits package. It's
about the example you set when no one's making you show up.

Next: Chapter 4 will explore the boss who promised confidentiality and delivered betrayal. Because your word is your currency, and
broken trust takes years to rebuild.

Chapter Four

The
Trust-Breaker

I f the email hacker taught me that control destroys trust, the hot-headed boss taught me that volume doesn't equal value, the absentee king taught me that you can't demand what you don't model, and the trust breaker taught me that your word is your currency and once you devalue it, you can't get it back.

The Assurance

I had concerns about someone on the team. Not performance issues, but leadership concerns. How they were managing people, the decisions they were making, the culture they were creating in their area. The kind of concerns that need to be raised but handled carefully.

I initially raised these concerns with the individual. Privately. I was bluntly told to "mind my own business and to stay in my lane". So I went to our boss. Privately. I sent him an email outlining the issues, then followed up with an in-person conversation. I wasn't trying to backstab anyone. I was trying to raise legitimate concerns through the appropriate channel.

He listened. Nodded. Assured me that the conversation was completely confidential. Just between the two of us. He understood the sensitivity. He'd handle it appropriately. Then, to prove his point, he picked up the printed copy of my email and tore it up. Right there in front of me. Into pieces. Demonstrative. Symbolic. A physical representation of his commitment to confidentiality.

"See?" he said. "This stays between us. You can trust me." I believed him.

The Betrayal

Fifteen minutes later, the person I'd raised concerns about showed up at my desk. They were holding my email. Not torn up pieces. The actual email. Printed. With my name on it. Every word I'd written.

"We need to talk about this," they said.

My boss had shown them everything. Not a summary. Not a vague "some concerns have been raised." My actual email. My exact words. My name attached. The person who'd just torn up the paper to prove confidentiality had apparently printed another copy the moment I left his office. The symbolic gesture meant nothing. The promise meant nothing. My trust meant nothing.

I stood there, feeling exposed and foolish. Betrayed by someone who'd made a show of protecting my confidence while planning to violate it before I'd even left the room.

The Aftermath

The anger came first. White-hot, immediate rage at being lied to so blatantly. He'd looked me in the eye, torn up the paper, promised confidentiality, and then immediately broken that promise. Not accidentally. Not under pressure. Deliberately, within minutes. He had no intention of keeping our conversation private. He'd lied to my face!

Then came the embarrassment. I'd been naive enough to believe him. The theatrical paper-tearing should have been a red flag. People who keep confidence don't need to perform it. They just do it. Underneath both emotions was something more permanent: resolve. I would never trust that boss again. Not with information, not with vulnerability, not with anything that mattered. The relationship was functionally over. I'd stay in my role, do my job, but the possibility of genuine followership was gone. That day I swore I would never do this to someone else.

What I Learned

- **Trust takes years to build and seconds to destroy.** I'd been working under this boss for months. Built what I thought was a reasonable working relationship. Thought we had enough trust for me to raise concerns safely. He destroyed all of that in fifteen minutes. You don't get to rebuild what you've shattered. You just live with the wreckage.

- **Symbolic gestures mean nothing without integrity.** The paper-tearing was theater. A performance designed to convince me without requiring actual trustworthiness. It worked, briefly, but actions always reveal truth. He tore up the paper and kept the email. The symbol was a lie covering the betrayal he'd already planned.

- **Your word has to actually mean something.** When he said "this stays between us," those words needed to create an obligation he felt bound by. Instead, they were just sounds that made me feel safe while he did what he wanted. Words without integrity are just manipulation.

- **People need to know their confidence is safe with you.** Not just believe it in theory. Know it through experience, because the moment they learn you betrayed someone else's trust, they'll never share anything real with you again. They'll give you the sanitized version, the politically safe version, the version that can't hurt them when you inevitably share it.

- **Once you betray trust, you rarely get it back.** He tried, later. Tried to rebuild the relationship. Tried to explain that he'd "handled it" by talking directly to the person, that transparency was important, that I should understand his position. None of it mattered. The trust was gone and without trust, everything else is just performance.

How I Lead Differently

That betrayal shaped how I handle trust more than almost any other experience.

- **I keep confidence religiously.** When someone shares something in confidence, it stays in confidence. Not "mostly in confidence" or "in confidence except for this one person who needs to know." In confidence. Period. I don't share it, don't hint at it, don't use it for political advantage, don't let it "accidentally" slip in any way. If someone needs to know, I go back to the person who confided in me and ask permission. "I think we need to bring this to X. Are you comfortable with that?" I don't make that call unilaterally. Their trust is more valuable than my convenience.

- **I mean what I say.** If I tell someone I'll do something, I do it. If I commit to confidentiality, I keep it. If I make a promise, I honor it. Not because I'm naturally trustworthy, but because I watched what happens when your word means nothing. People stop believing you. They stop sharing real information. They stop following authentically. All you're left with is compliance and political maneuvering.

- **I don't make symbolic gestures.** I don't tear up papers. I don't make dramatic shows of trustworthiness. I just keep confidence, consistently, over time. Trust isn't built through performance. It's built through pattern. People learn to trust you by watching what you do when no one's forcing you to be trustworthy.

- **I'm careful about what I commit to.** I won't promise confidentiality if I know the information will require action that breaks it. I won't say "this stays between us" if there's a chance it can't. Better to be honest up front, "I can't promise complete confidentiality because if this is X, I'll have to involve Y," than to make a promise I can't keep.

The Biblical Foundation

Scripture treats trustworthiness as foundational to character:

Matthew 5:37 "Let what you say be simply 'Yes' or 'No'; anything more than this comes from evil."

Your yes should mean yes. Your no should mean no. You shouldn't need elaborate promises or symbolic gestures to prove you'll keep your word. Your word itself should be sufficient because your character backs it up. That boss needed to tear up the paper because his word alone wasn't credible. The performance was compensation for lack of integrity. If his "this stays between us" actually meant something, he wouldn't have needed theater to convince me.

Proverbs 11:13 "Whoever goes about slandering reveals secrets, but he who is trustworthy in spirit keeps a thing covered."

Trustworthiness isn't about what you say. It's about what you keep covered. Do people's secrets stay secret with you? Do confidences stay confidential? Or do you use information for your own advantage?

Proverbs 25:9 "Argue your case with your neighbor himself, and do not reveal another's secret, lest he who hears you bring shame upon you, and your ill repute have no end."

When you break confidence, you don't just damage the relationship with the person you betrayed. You damage your reputation with everyone who hears about it. Your "ill repute has no end" because everyone learns they can't trust you.

> **Psalm 15:1-4** "who swears to his own hurt and does not change."

Keep your promises even when it costs you. Honor your commitments even when breaking them would be convenient. Your word should bind you even when circumstances change.

That boss broke his word the moment it became convenient. He promised confidentiality, then immediately violated it because directly confronting the person with my email seemed easier than handling it diplomatically. Convenience trumped commitment, and in doing so, he proved his word was worthless.

The Secular Case

You don't need Scripture to understand why broken trust destroys leadership:

- **Information flow stops.** When people know you can't be trusted with sensitive information, they stop sharing it. You get the sanitized version, the safe version, the version that won't hurt them if you betray them. You lose access to the real problems, the actual concerns, the information you need to lead effectively. Everyone becomes a political operator, managing what you know rather than helping you understand reality.

- **Good people leave.** High performers don't stick around to be betrayed. They go somewhere their trust will be honored.

You're left with people who either can't leave or have learned to operate in environments of broken trust. Neither group builds great organizations.

- **Crisis response collapses.** When things go wrong, people need to feel safe raising alarms. If they know you'll expose them, throw them under the bus, or break confidence when pressure hits, they'll stay quiet until the problem becomes catastrophic. You don't find out about issues until they're disasters.

- **Culture becomes toxic.** Broken trust spreads. When people see you betray one person, everyone becomes more guarded. They start protecting themselves instead of collaborating. Politics replace honesty. Self-preservation replaces mission focus. The whole organization optimizes for safety rather than effectiveness.

- **Your influence evaporates.** Leadership without trust is just authority. People comply because they have to, not because they believe in you or the mission. They do the minimum required. They don't give discretionary effort. They certainly don't follow you into anything difficult or risky. Why would they? You've proven you'll sacrifice them for your convenience.

My Rough Edges

I wish I could tell you that experience made me perfectly trustworthy. But the truth is more complicated.

- **My nature is to be an open book.** I tend to trust people really quickly and thus am willing to share nearly everything. Over time I have been burned several times, outside of this instance, which has led me to hold back when I should be open.

- **I struggle to extend trust after being burned.** That boss taught me that people will look you in the eye and lie. That symbolic gestures can cover betrayal. That promises don't always bind behavior. Now, when someone asks me to trust them, part of me holds back. I want evidence. I want pattern. I want proof over time. That's probably wise. But sometimes it crosses into cynicism. Sometimes I withhold trust that people have earned because I'm protecting myself from being fooled again.

- **I'm overly cautious about what I share.** Even with people who've proven trustworthy, I find myself calculating risk. "If I tell them this, what happens if they share it?" I don't assume betrayal, but I'm always aware of the possibility. That caution probably protects me. It also probably prevents deeper relationships than I'd have if I were more willing to be vulnerable.

- **I test people's trustworthiness sometimes.** Not consciously, not deliberately, but I notice myself sharing small things to see if they stay confidential. Watching to see if information I shared with one person shows up in another conversation. Checking whether promises get kept on small things before I trust them with big things. That's not necessarily wrong. Trust should be earned and proven over time, but sometimes I realize I'm running tests people don't know they're taking and that's not quite fair.

- **I'm tempted toward cynicism about others' promises.** When someone makes an emphatic promise, part of me thinks "Yeah, we'll see." When someone assures me of confidentiality, I remember the torn-up paper and wonder what they're hiding. I have to consciously fight against assuming everyone will betray trust the way that boss did, because the truth is, most people aren't that boss. Most people mean what they say. Most people keep confidence when they promise it. One dramatic betrayal taught me to question everyone and that's not entirely healthy.

The Reputation You Build

Here's what I learned from watching trust break and trying to build it myself: Your reputation for trustworthiness is built in a thousand small moments. Every time you keep confidence when sharing it would benefit you. Every time you honor a promise when breaking it would be convenient. Every time you protect someone who trusted you with something vulnerable.

No one moment builds that reputation. But the pattern does. When that boss tore up my email and then immediately betrayed me, he destroyed his reputation in one moment. He'd probably been building toward that moment for a while. I just hadn't seen it yet. The theatrical gesture wasn't out of character. It was revealing of character.

People are always watching. Not just in the big moments, but in the small ones. How you handle the information someone shares casually. Whether you keep promises on minor things. How you talk about people who aren't in the room. All of it builds a pattern and that pattern determines whether people trust you when it really matters.

The Choice Every Leader Makes

You can be trustworthy, or you can be convenient. You can't reliably be both. Keeping confidence is often inconvenient. It would be easier to share information that makes you look good. It would be simpler to break a promise that's become costly. It would be more comfortable to betray trust than to honor it when pressure mounts.

Trustworthy leaders choose the inconvenient path. They keep confidence even when sharing would help them. They honor promises even when breaking them would be easier. They protect trust even when violating it would be convenient. Your team already knows which kind of leader you are. Not based on what you promise. Based on what they've watched you do. Based on the pattern you've built over time. Based on whether your word binds your behavior or just manages perception.

That boss taught me what broken trust looks like. The theatrical gesture covering immediate betrayal. The symbolic promise masking selfish action. The word that meant nothing because it cost nothing to break. I've tried to build the opposite. Not perfectly. Not without struggles, but consistently. Because I know what it feels like to have your trust betrayed and I swore I'd never make someone else feel that way. Your word is your currency. Spend it carefully. Honor it completely. Once people learn it's worthless, you can't buy it back.

Next: Chapter 5 will synthesize the lessons from these four bad bosses into the framework that shaped everything that came after. Pain is the best teacher, but only if you learn from it.

Chapter Five

The Pattern in the Pain

F our bad bosses. Four different failures. Four lessons burned into my leadership through experience I wouldn't wish on anyone. Pain, it turns out, is an excellent teacher. Not because it feels good, but because it forces you to build something better. When you watch trust destroyed, you learn why trust matters. When you see ego blind someone to reality, you learn why humility is essential. When you experience absent leadership, you learn why presence can't be outsourced. When your confidence is betrayed, you learn why your word has to mean something.

Over eighteen years, watching these leaders fail in different ways, I built a framework. Not consciously at first. Not systematically, but piece by piece, failure by failure, I started to see patterns. Principles that held when everything else collapsed. Questions that cut through complexity. A way of making decisions that didn't fall apart under pressure.

I built this framework before I became a Christian. Through trial and error. Through watching what destroyed teams and what built them. Through experiencing the cost of bad leadership and swearing I'd never inflict that cost on someone else. Then, after I gave my life to Christ, I discovered something that stopped me cold. The framework I'd built through pain was Biblical.

Not because I'd been trying to follow Scripture. I hadn't. But because the Bible describes reality accurately. The principles that work, work because they're true, and truth shows up whether you're looking for it in Scripture or discovering it through the wreckage of bad leadership.

The Four-Part Framework

Here's what emerged from watching those four bosses fail:

1. Humility: "Who Am I to Judge? What Am I Missing?"

The hotheaded boss taught me this through negative example. His ego blinded him to his own limitations. He couldn't see that his encryption scheme was a disaster because admitting he was wrong would threaten his identity. He yelled at people who tried to help him because accepting input meant accepting he didn't have all the answers.

I learned: Start with humility. Assume you're missing something. Ask "What don't I see?" before asking "What should I do?" Check your motives. Examine your blind spots. Recognize that being smart about one thing doesn't make you right about everything.

Humility isn't weakness. It's accuracy. It's seeing yourself clearly enough to lead effectively. It's creating space for wisdom to come from

anywhere, not just from you. The question isn't "Am I smart enough
to solve this?" The question is "Am I humble enough to find the best
solution, even if it's not mine?"

2. Whole Counsel: "What's the Complete Human and Business Impact?"

The absentee king taught me this. He optimized for his own comfort
and convenience, never considering the impact on the team. When the
production outage hit and he wasn't there, he wasn't thinking about
the human cost, the client impact, the message his absence sent. He
was thinking about himself.

I learned: See the full picture. Who does this affect? What are the
human consequences, not just the business outcomes? What's at stake
for the people involved, for the organization, for the mission?

Whole counsel means understanding that decisions ripple. The
junior analyst (Chapter 6) wasn't just "someone who made a mistake."
She was someone on a work visa supporting her family, shaking and
terrified, facing a moment that could destroy her life. The inappropriate employee (Chapter 7) wasn't just "someone causing problems." He
was someone with potential AND a pattern of harm affecting women
who deserved safety.

The question isn't "What's convenient?" The question is "What's
the complete impact of this decision on everyone it touches?"

3. Restoration or Protection: "Can This Be Fixed, or Does Someone Need Defending?"

All four bosses taught me this in different ways. The email hacker who
couldn't trust created environments people wanted to escape from

instead of cultures worth building. The hotheaded boss who couldn't admit mistakes destroyed opportunities for growth. The absentee king who wouldn't model expectations created resentment instead of followership. The trust breaker who wouldn't keep confidence destroyed safety instead of building it.

I learned: Ask the right question. Can this person or situation be restored? Is this a mistake that can be corrected, or a pattern that's causing harm? Does someone need grace to grow, or do vulnerable people need protection from ongoing damage?

This isn't about being soft or hard. It's about being wise. Grace when restoration is possible. Protection when harm is continuing. Same framework, different applications depending on context. The question isn't "How do I feel about this?" The question is "What does this situation actually require?"

4. Moral Intuition: "Does This Feel Right Based on Principles, Not Politics?"

The trust breaker taught me this most powerfully. When he tore up that paper and then immediately showed my email to the person I'd raised concerns about, he chose political convenience over principled action. What was expedient over what was right. What served him over what honored trust.

I learned: Check your gut, but check it against principles. Does this decision align with what you actually believe, or is it compromised by fear, pressure, or politics? Are you doing this because it's right, or because it's convenient? Because it serves the mission, or because it protects you?

Moral intuition isn't just feelings. It's your internal sense of whether a decision aligns with principles you've tested over time.

When something feels wrong, that's data. When you're rationalizing, that's a warning sign. When you'd be embarrassed to explain your reasoning out loud, you probably shouldn't do it. The question isn't "Can I justify this?" The question is "Does this align with who I want to be and what I actually believe?"

The Framework in Practice

This isn't a formula that spits out answers. It's a way of thinking through complex decisions when the right choice isn't obvious. Let me show you what this framework would have looked like if those four bad bosses had actually used it:

The Email Hacker could have run through the framework before installing surveillance:

- **Humility:** Am I monitoring people because they're untrustworthy, or because I'm insecure?

- **Whole Counsel:** How will surveillance affect team morale, trust, and psychological safety?

- **Restoration or Protection:** Do I need to protect the company from bad employees, or do I need to build trust with good ones?

- **Moral Intuition:** Does treating people like criminals align with the kind of leader I want to be?

If he'd asked those questions, he wouldn't have hacked my email. He'd have built trust instead of destroying it.

The Hotheaded Boss could have run through it before pushing his encryption disaster:

- **Humility:** Am I right about this, or is my ego preventing me from seeing the problems?

- **Whole Counsel:** What happens to our security, our clients, our team if this encryption scheme fails?

- **Restoration or Protection:** Do I need to protect my idea, or do I need to protect the company from a bad technical decision?

- **Moral Intuition:** Does yelling at people who question me align with my principles, or just my ego?

If he'd asked those questions, he might have accepted input and avoided the security disaster.

The Absentee King could have run through it before claiming work-from-home privileges:

- **Humility:** Am I special enough to deserve different rules, or am I just making excuses?

- **Whole Counsel:** How does my absence affect team morale, crisis response, and culture?

- **Restoration or Protection:** Am I protecting my comfort, or am I building an environment where people want to stay?

- **Moral Intuition:** Does claiming privileges I deny others align with the kind of leader I claim to be?

If he'd asked those questions, he'd have been present when the production outage hit.

The Trust Breaker could have run through it before showing my email:

- **Humility:** Is breaking confidence the right call, or just the convenient one?

- **Whole Counsel:** What happens to trust, safety, and information flow if I betray this confidence?

- **Restoration or Protection:** Do I need to protect political convenience, or do I need to honor the trust someone placed in me?

- **Moral Intuition:** Does breaking a promise fifteen minutes after making it align with having integrity?

If he'd asked those questions, he wouldn't have destroyed trust that took months to build.

The framework works by forcing you to think clearly when pressure, ego, convenience, or politics are pushing you toward bad decisions. It doesn't guarantee you'll choose correctly. But it makes the choice clear.

The Biblical Discovery

Years after building this framework through painful experience, I became a Christian and as I started reading Scripture, something remarkable happened. I kept seeing my framework. Then the realization hit me, humbling and profound: This wasn't my framework at all.

What I'd thought I built through my own observation and hard-earned wisdom was actually God, in His infinite wisdom, allowing me to see His work at play. The principles I'd "discovered" through eighteen years of trial and error weren't mine. They were His. Always had been. I was just finally reading the instruction manual for what He'd already written into reality itself.

I hadn't invented anything. I'd just stumbled onto truth that had been there all along, waiting to be recognized. Truth that was woven into the fabric of how He designed leadership, organizations, and human flourishing to actually work.

Humility:

> Proverbs 11:2 "When pride comes, then comes disgrace, but with the humble is wisdom."

> James 4:6 says "God opposes the proud but gives grace to the humble."

The whole Bible treats humility not as optional niceness, but as essential to seeing clearly and leading well.

Whole Counsel:

> Proverbs 31:8-9 calls leaders to consider impact on the vulnerable: "Open your mouth for the mute, for the rights of all who are destitute. Open your mouth, judge righteously, defend the rights of the poor and needy."

Leadership requires seeing the complete picture, especially those most affected by decisions.

Restoration or Protection:

Matthew 18:15-17 gives a process: try restoration first,
but protect the community when restoration fails.

Galatians 6:1-5 addresses both sides: "restore him in
a spirit of gentleness" (verse 1), but also "each one
should carry their own load" (verse 5).

Grace when appropriate, accountability when necessary.
Moral Intuition:

Proverbs 3:5-6 says "Trust in the Lord with all your
heart, and do not lean on your own understanding.
In all your ways acknowledge him, and he will make
straight your paths."

Moral intuition grounded in principles, not just feelings or politics.
Conviction over convenience. I didn't build this framework by trying
to be Biblical. I built it by trying not to be like those bad bosses. By
watching what destroyed teams and building the opposite. By learning from pain what actually works. Then I discovered it was Biblical
anyway.

Why This Matters

This is the point that both Christian and secular leaders need to understand:

- **For secular leaders:** These principles work whether you believe the Bible or not. They work because they describe how reality actually functions. How humans actually respond. How organizations actually thrive or collapse. The Bible isn't a religious text disconnected from real life. It's an accurate description of how the world works. Which means the principles it teaches work whether you believe their source or not.

- **For Christian leaders:** The fact that I built this framework before faith proves something crucial. You don't need to make your leadership "Christian" by adding religious language or creating Christian subcultures at work. Biblical principles ARE practical principles. They show up in leadership that works, whether the leader acknowledges their source or not. Your job isn't to Christianize your workplace. It's to lead so well, from such clear convictions, that people ask why you're different.

- **For everyone:** This framework holds because it's true. Not true because I believe it, or true because it's in the Bible, but true because it describes reality accurately. When you lead with humility, you see more clearly. When you consider whole counsel, you make better decisions. When you choose restoration or protection wisely, you build stronger teams. When you follow moral intuition grounded in principles, you create cultures of integrity.

- Truth works. Even when you don't recognize its source. Even when you're just trying to avoid being a bad boss. Even when you're building through pain without a blueprint.

Common Grace

Theologians call this "common grace." The idea that God reveals truth to everyone, not just those who follow him. That reality itself reflects how God designed things to work. That you don't need special revelation to see that humility is better than ego, that integrity matters, that grace and accountability both have their place.

The framework I built through pain was common grace at work. God revealing truth through reality itself. Through the natural consequences of good and bad leadership. Through watching what destroyed teams and what built them. Through eighteen years of learning that some principles hold and others collapse.

I didn't know I was discovering Biblical principles. I thought I was just learning to lead well. But it turns out those are the same thing. Because the God who wrote Scripture also designed reality. And when you pay attention to how reality actually works, you end up discovering what Scripture has been saying all along.

The principles work because they're true. They're in the Bible because the Bible tells the truth about how reality functions. And anyone willing to learn from experience, to let pain teach them, to build something better from wreckage, can discover these truths whether they ever open Scripture or not.

What Comes Next

I've shown you the education of pain. Four bad bosses who taught me what not to do. I've shown you the framework that emerged from that wreckage. Now comes the hard part: showing you what this framework looks like under real pressure. Not in theory. Not in principle. In actual decisions where real things are at stake. Where the right choice isn't obvious. Where principles collide and you have to figure out which one matters most. Where your framework either holds or collapses.

The next chapters will show you this framework in action. Sometimes I'll apply it correctly and the outcome will prove the framework works. Sometimes I'll compromise under pressure and the outcome will prove the framework works by showing what happens when you violate it. The framework doesn't fail. You do. I do. We all do.

When you have a framework you've tested, that's proven over time, that aligns with how reality actually works, you can make the hard calls and sleep at night. Not because you're always right, but because you're consistently principled. In leadership, that's what builds cultures where people feel safe, where excellence matters, and where trust becomes the foundation for everything else you're trying to build. Let me show you how it works.

Next: Part 2 begins with Chapter 6: Grace Under Fire. Where a junior analyst makes a catastrophic mistake, and the framework has to work in real time with real consequences.

Part 2

P rinciples are easy to believe when nothing's at stake. The test comes when the pressure's on, the costs are real, and the easy path and the right path diverge.

This section shows you the framework under fire. A junior analyst deletes production data and the pressure to fire her is overwhelming. An inappropriate employee has to be removed after three chances, and grace has to give way to protection. A sales meeting where correcting lies in front of a client could cost us the deal. A $350,000 billing mistake where I failed to follow my own framework and paid the price.

These aren't sanitized case studies. They're real decisions with real consequences. Real people whose lives hung in the balance. Real business impact measured in hundreds of thousands of dollars. Real moments where what I chose revealed whether my framework was real or just words I said when it was convenient.

Sometimes I applied the framework correctly and the outcome proved it works. Sometimes I violated it under pressure and the outcome proved it works by showing what gets destroyed when you ignore it, because the framework doesn't fail. You do. I do. We all do.

When you have a framework tested under pressure, when you've seen it hold in crisis and watched what happens when you compromise it, you learn something more valuable than theory. You learn what's actually true about people, trust, and leadership. Not what sounds good in a book, but what holds when everything else is falling apart. Let me show you how it works when the stakes are real.

Chapter Six

Grace Under Fire

The Microsoft Teams call came at 2:47 PM on a Tuesday. One of my business analysts was on the other end, voice tight with panic.

"Justin, we have a problem. Production environment. They were testing in production by mistake."

My stomach dropped before I even heard the rest. I knew what was coming.

"How bad?"

"Bad. Payments deleted. Transactions voided. She was cleaning up test data... except it wasn't test data."

She. I already knew who it was before they said her name. The junior analyst we'd hired eight months ago. Smart, dedicated, meticulous, and now absolutely terrified because she'd just made the kind of mistake that ends careers.

The Situation

Let's call her Priya. Mid-twenties, on an H-1B work visa from India. She'd just brought her entire family over to the United States: mom, dad, brother, and sister. She was the only one working. This job wasn't just her livelihood, it was theirs. Their entire American dream was riding on her paycheck.

She was genuinely good at her job. Smart. Dedicated. Outspoken. The kind of person who stayed late to make sure things were done right, who asked thoughtful and tough questions, who cared deeply about quality. She'd been so careful, so thorough in everything she did, always double-checking her work. Until today.

She'd run a cleanup script in what she thought was the development environment. Standard QA procedure: delete test payments, void fake transactions, reset the data for the next round of testing. Except her terminal was pointed at production and by the time she realized it, real customer payments were gone and legitimate transactions were voided.

Here's what made it worse: We had backups. We could restore the data. That wasn't the problem. The problem was that when you delete a payment in our system, it automatically sends a notification to the bank to void and stop payment on the associated checks. Which means we'd just triggered bank-level actions on real checks going to real people: healthcare providers, vendors, contractors, people who were counting on those payments to clear.

This wasn't just a data cleanup issue. It was going to impact real people with real financial problems if we couldn't unwind it fast enough. The damage was fixable, but time-consuming. Stressful for clients. Expensive in terms of engineering hours. And potentially damaging to real people's finances and our client relationships. The kind of mistake that makes executives start drafting termination paperwork.

When I got on the call with her, she was clearly shaken. I could see it in her face on the video. Her voice was barely above a whisper when she tried to explain what happened. She kept apologizing, over and over, eyes filling with tears she was fighting to hold back. The next call, with senior leadership, had a very different energy.

The Pressure

"She needs to go. Today." The VP of Operations wasn't asking. He was declaring. He wasn't alone.

"This is exactly the kind of carelessness we can't tolerate."

"If we don't make an example, what message does that send?"

"Production testing? That's QA 101. She should know better."

They weren't wrong on the facts. It *was* careless. It *did* cost us. Yes, any QA analyst worth their salt knows you never, ever test in production. The technical failure was clear. The business impact was real. Everyone on that call was looking at me to deliver the consequences.

Part of me agreed with them. She'd violated a fundamental rule. The kind of rule that exists specifically to prevent exactly this scenario. We had processes. We had safeguards. She'd bypassed all of them, probably rushing, probably not paying attention, and now we were all paying for it.

Here's what no one was saying out loud: As the CTO, this was also *my* fault. A junior analyst shouldn't have had access to the production environment in the first place. That's a basic security and operational principle. I'd failed to properly lock down our environments. I'd failed to implement proper role-based access controls. The system that allowed her to make this mistake was a system I'd designed and failed to properly restrict.

This was the perfect opportunity to "send a message" to the rest of the team about the importance of being careful. About following procedures. About the consequences of costly mistakes. The case for termination practically made itself. Firing her would also conveniently let me off the hook for my own leadership failure.

The Framework Applied

Something in my gut was screaming that firing her would be the wrong call. I asked everyone to give me twenty minutes before we made any final decisions. I needed to think through this properly, not just react to the pressure.

Humility: "Who am I to judge?"

The first question I asked myself was simple: *Had I ever made this exact mistake?*

Yes. Multiple times. Early in my career, I'd deleted an entire production databases. Not just records, an entire database. Gone. The first time it happened, I was maybe two years into professional development, and I spent the next six hours in a cold sweat while we restored from backups. The second time, I had less of an excuse. I just wasn't paying attention, got my terminal windows mixed up, and boom. Production down.

I'd been given grace both times. My boss could have fired me. Probably should have, by the standard being proposed in that conference call. Instead, he taught me. Showed me how to set up terminal color schemes so dev and prod environments were visually distinct. Helped me build better habits. Turned a catastrophic mistake into a learning experience.

If I'd been fired for doing the exact same thing Priya just did, I wouldn't have been around to build the systems and teams I'd built over the next sixteen years. *Who am I to judge her more harshly than I was judged?*

There was another layer of humility I had to face: This wasn't just her mistake. It was mine too. As the CTO, I shouldn't have given a junior analyst access to production in the first place. That's Systems Administration 101. Role-based access control. Principle of least privilege. All the security fundamentals I knew and preached about. I'd failed to properly implement them. She'd made an execution error. I'd made a *design* error.

If I fired her, I'd be punishing her for a mistake I'd enabled by not building proper guardrails into the system. I'd be making her the scapegoat for my own leadership failure. The question became sharper: *Am I pushing for her termination because she violated policy, or because firing her is easier than admitting I built a flawed system?*

Whole Counsel: "What's the complete impact?"

The business impact was real. I wasn't minimizing that. We'd lost time, money, and client confidence. Worse, we'd triggered bank notifications that could affect real people's finances, healthcare providers waiting for payments, vendors who'd already shipped products, contractors counting on those checks. That mattered.

There was also a human being on the other end of that call whose entire life was about to be destroyed if I said the word. She was on a work visa. Losing this job didn't just mean finding another one, it meant potentially having to leave the country. Her visa was tied to employment. No job meant no visa. No visa meant going back to India, away from the life she'd built, the career she was growing.

It wasn't just her. She'd just moved her entire family to the US: mom, dad, brother, and sister. She was the only one with a wage right now. They were completely dependent on her income. Not money she was sending back home to India, they were *here*, in America, building a new life, and she was the only thing standing between them and financial disaster.

This job wasn't just her career. It was her family's entire foundation in a new country. I thought about her on that video call, shaking, voice trembling, fighting back tears. She wasn't defiant. She wasn't making excuses. She was terrified because she understood the magnitude of what she'd done and what it could cost her. The question became: *What's more valuable? Making an example, or making a person?*

Restoration: "Can this be fixed?"

The data could be restored. That was the easy part. Yes, it was time-consuming, but fixable. The harder question: Could *she* be restored? Was this a pattern of carelessness, or a one-time mistake? Everything I knew about her work up to this point said it was the latter. She'd been meticulous. Detail-oriented. This wasn't a person who routinely cut corners or ignored procedures. This was someone who'd made one catastrophic error.

There's a difference between incompetence and inexperience. Incompetence can't be fixed; you either have the capacity or you don't. Inexperience can absolutely be fixed, it just requires teaching instead of punishment. This was clearly a teaching moment, not a termination moment.

If I fired her, I'd lose the opportunity to help her become the kind of junior analyst who never makes this mistake again. She'd carry the shame of this failure into whatever came next, without the redemption of learning from it. If I kept her, I could turn this into the defining moment of her career. The moment she learned to be excellent under pressure, to build better habits, and to understand why processes exist.

Moral Intuition: "Does this feel right?"

Stripping away the business jargon and the pressure from other executives, I had to ask: *Does destroying this person's life over an honest mistake align with who I want to be as a leader?*

It didn't.

Yes, there were consequences. Yes, it cost us, but she wasn't malicious. She wasn't negligent in the sense of not caring. She made an error, a significant one, but the kind of error that anyone could make if they weren't careful enough for five seconds. The punishment didn't fit the crime. Firing her would be disproportionate to the offense. It would be choosing severity over wisdom. Choosing to make an example over making a difference. Every part of my framework was pointing the same direction: This was a moment for grace, not judgment.

The Outcome

I joined the Teams call with the C-level executives.

"We're not firing her."

The VP of Operations looked like I'd just told him we were giving everyone free cars.

"What? Justin, you can't be serious."

"I'm completely serious. We're going to treat this as a teaching moment. She's going to learn from this, and she's going to be better because of it."

"What message does that send to the rest of the team?"

"That we care more about developing our people than we do about performative discipline. That mistakes are opportunities to improve, not automatic career death sentences."

I won't pretend it was a popular decision. Several executives on that call thought I was being soft. Making a mistake. Setting a dangerous precedent. I got back on a call with Priya, and had a very different conversation than she was expecting.

"You made a significant mistake today. You know that. I know that. I want you to know, I've made the exact same mistake. More than once. Someone gave me grace when I didn't deserve it, and it changed my career. So here's what's going to happen: You're going to help fix this. You're going to document what went wrong. You're going to build safeguards so it never happens again. Not just for you, for everyone."

The relief on her face was immediate, but it was mixed with something else: determination.

Short-Term Results

She never made that mistake again. Not because she was afraid of being fired, but because she'd experienced grace and didn't want to waste it. She became meticulous about environment checks. Started color-coding her terminals. Built checklists, and more importantly, she started teaching other people on the team the lessons she'd learned.

Her performance didn't just recover, it improved. She double-checked everything. Took ownership of quality in a way she hadn't before. The mistake became the foundation of excellence. She went on to fix this process, and many others. She added safeguards to the script so if it detected it was running in production it would short circuit rather than execute. She wrote standard operating procedures that we still use to this day.

I fixed the systemic problem too. Within the week, I'd locked down production access. Implemented proper role-based permissions. Made it so junior analysts *couldn't* accidentally test in production, even if they wanted to. The guardrails I should have built from the beginning were finally in place.

Two people learned from one mistake: She learned to be more careful. I learned to build better systems.

Long-Term Impact

One month later, we had to do a round of layoffs to right-size the company. Budget cuts, reorganization, the usual corporate casualties. When it came time to decide who stayed and who went, Priya survived. Not just because of her technical skills, but because of the loyalty and excellence she'd demonstrated after that production incident. Others with clean records but less demonstrated commitment didn't make the cut.

Five months after that, we lost our largest client. The financial hit was massive. We had no choice but to make deeper cuts, and this time, Priya was part of the reduction. Not because of her performance, she was still excellent. Simply because we didn't have the money to keep the team at that size.

Here's where the grace from that production incident paid dividends in a different way:

We went to war for her.

Reference letters. LinkedIn recommendations. Personal introductions to other companies that needed junior analysts. We worked our network to help her land quickly. She got a small severance package to help support her family during the transition, something we didn't do for most others who were let go.

The people who hadn't built that kind of relationship with us? We gave them the standard two weeks and a handshake. Priya got a team of people actively fighting to make sure she landed safely. That's what grace builds: not just loyalty in the moment, but a relationship that holds even when circumstances force hard decisions.

She found another position within three weeks. Better pay. Better title. She stayed in touch, grateful for how we'd handled both the production incident and the layoff. The grace we showed her when she made a mistake created a foundation of trust that lasted beyond her employment with us.

The Biblical Foundation

I was already a Christian when this happened. I'd been studying Scripture seriously for a while by then. As I worked through the decision about Priya, these Biblical principles weren't something I discovered later. They were actively shaping my thinking in the moment.

> **Romans 2:4** "God's kindness is meant to lead you to repentance."

Not His judgment. Not His punishment. His *kindness*. That verse was running through my head as I thought about how to handle Priya. If God's strategy for changing people is kindness, not severity, why would I think fear-based punishment would be more effective?

When Paul writes to the Galatians about dealing with someone who's fallen into sin, he doesn't say "fire them immediately." He says, "Brothers, if anyone is caught in any transgression, you who are spiritual should restore him in a spirit of gentleness" (Galatians 6:1)

Restore. Not destroy. The goal isn't punishment, it's restoration.

> **Ephesians 4:32** "Be kind to one another, tender-
> hearted, forgiving one another, as God in Christ for-
> gave you."

That last phrase is the key: *as God in Christ forgave you.*

If I'd been held to the standard I was being pressured to hold
Priya to (zero tolerance for costly mistakes), I wouldn't have a career.
I wouldn't have a faith, for that matter. I'd have been fired a dozen
times over for the mistakes I made learning how to be good at what I
do. Spiritually? I'd be in far worse shape if God had given me what I
deserved instead of what I needed.

Grace isn't just nice. It's *strategic*. It's how people actually grow and
improve.

> **Proverbs 24:16** "The righteous falls seven times and
> rises again."

The assumption in Scripture is that good people will fail. Repeatedly. What distinguishes the righteous isn't perfection? Resilience.
The capacity to get back up and keep going. You can only rise again
if someone doesn't kick you while you're down.

The Secular Translation

If the Bible doesn't resonate with you, let me put it in business terms:
psychological safety is one of the strongest predictors of high-per-
forming teams.

Google's Project Aristotle (a massive study of what makes teams effective) found that the number one factor wasn't intelligence, or skill, or resources. It was psychological safety: the belief that you can take risks, make mistakes, speak up, and challenge ideas without being punished or humiliated for it.

Grace isn't weakness. It's *strategic investment in performance.*

When people feel safe to fail, they:

- Take smarter risks instead of playing it safe

- Report problems early instead of hiding them

- Learn faster because they're not defensive

- Stay loyal when other opportunities come along

- Innovate more because they're not paralyzed by fear

Firing Priya would have sent a message to the entire team: One mistake and you're done. Don't take risks. Protect yourself. Blame someone else if things go wrong. Keeping her sent a different message: We care more about who you become than who you were when you failed.

That's not soft leadership. That's building a culture where people can become excellent because they're not wasting energy protecting themselves from their own team. The business case for grace is simple: People who experience it perform better. They stay longer. They give more. They build stronger teams. Grace isn't just morally right. It's *practically effective.*

The Hard Truth

I'd love to tell you this was easy. That I joined that C-level call with complete confidence and zero doubt. That's not what happened. Part of me was angry. Part of me thought they were right. She should have known better, she should have been more careful, and maybe making an example would prevent future mistakes. Part of me was worried about my own reputation. What if other executives thought I was soft? What if this backfired and she made another mistake? What if keeping her made me look weak?

The framework didn't remove the pressure. It gave me a way to process it. Humility forced me to confront my own hypocrisy. I'd made the same mistake and been given grace. Whole counsel forced me to see her as a whole person, not just a liability. Restoration gave me a better option than punishment. Moral intuition, that gut-level sense of what's right, told me that destroying someone's life over an honest mistake violated something fundamental about how I wanted to lead.

The principles held. Even when it was uncomfortable. Even when it cost me political capital with other executives. That's the point of a framework: it works when your feelings don't. Leadership isn't just about making the easy calls when everyone agrees. It's about making the right calls when everyone's pressuring you to do the opposite.

The junior analyst situation taught me that the moments when you're most tempted to abandon your principles are exactly the moments when they matter most. People are watching. Not just to see what you do in that moment, but to figure out whether they can trust you in the next one. That trust, built through consistency over time, becomes the foundation for everything else you're trying to build. You can't buy it. You can't fake it. You can only earn it by proving, again and again, that your principles hold when the pressure's on.

Chapter Seven

When Protection Trumps Restoration

T he hardest part of having a leadership framework isn't applying it when the answer is obvious. It's applying it when the answer costs you something you care about.

I had an older employee who was rough around the edges. He was abrasive, crude, and carried the weight of a difficult upbringing in every interaction. I genuinely liked him. Once you got past the rough exterior, there was a good person underneath. I didn't hang out with him outside of work, but I enjoyed small doses of time with him and saw real potential.

Here's what made this even more complicated: He was one of the most gifted programmers I've ever worked with. Not just competent, but genuinely exceptional. He understood code from top to bottom and had that rare ability to see the holistic application, how all the pieces fit together. The kind of developer you build critical systems around. The kind of talent you don't just replace. Then the reports started coming in.

The Pattern

It wasn't a one-time mistake. Multiple women on our staff reported that he was being inappropriate and offensive with them. Different incidents, different women, same pattern of behavior.

Here's where it got complicated: Part of me didn't want to give up on him. I could see the good in him. I wanted to believe he could change. The same framework that led me to extend grace to the QA analyst who made an honest mistake was now forcing me to confront a much harder question. When does grace to one person become cruelty to everyone else?

Three Conversations

Conversation One: Just the two of us, alone on a Teams call. I laid out what had been reported, explained why it was unacceptable, and made it absolutely clear I would not tolerate it again. No ambiguity. This was a line he couldn't cross. I gave him a chance to change. That's what restoration looks like: you identify the problem, set clear expectations, and create space for different behavior. He said he understood. He'd be more careful.

Conversation Two: a month later, another report came in. Similar behavior, different woman. Enough time had passed that we decided to give him one more chance, but I escalated the tone significantly. This wasn't a coaching conversation anymore. This was last warning territory. We documented everything. He knew exactly where he stood.

Again, he said he understood. He'd change.

Conversation Three: A few weeks later, the third report removed all doubt. There was no real change happening. He might have been more careful for a few weeks after each conversation, but the pattern persisted. That conversation was short.

The Same Framework, A Different Outcome

Remember the decision framework:

- **Humility:** Recognize what you don't know and can't control

- **Whole Counsel:** See who this affects beyond the immediate situation

- **Restoration or Protection:** Can this be fixed, or does someone need defending?

- **Moral Intuition:** What does your conscience, shaped by wisdom, tell you is right?

With the junior analyst who made the mistake, the framework led to grace:

- **Humility:** I didn't know everything about her personal situation or the pressures she was under. I couldn't predict whether one mistake would define her career or become a turning point. I had to admit I'd made similar errors early in my own career.

- **Whole Counsel:** The impact was contained, the client relationship was salvageable, and the team was watching to see how I'd respond to honest failure.

- **Restoration or Protection:** She made an honest mistake, showed genuine remorse, and there was no pattern of harm. The question was: "Can this be fixed?" The answer was yes.

- **Moral Intuition:** Everything in me said this person deserved another chance. Grace felt right here.

With this employee, the framework led somewhere different:

- **Humility:** I had to admit my initial read on him was wrong. I'd hoped coaching would work. I'd believed his promises to change. But humility also meant accepting that my desire to see the best in him didn't change the reality of what he was doing.

- **Whole Counsel:** The women on my team deserved a workplace where they felt respected and safe. Their dignity wasn't negotiable. This wasn't just about him and me. It was about creating a culture where vulnerable people were protected, not exposed.

- **Restoration or Protection:** We tried restoration three times. Clear expectations, progressive discipline, multiple chances to change. But the pattern continued. At some point, hoping for change becomes ignoring harm. The question shifted from "Can this be fixed?" to "How long will we let this continue?"

- **Moral Intuition:** My personal feelings about liking this guy couldn't override the safety of my team. My discomfort with hard conversations couldn't matter more than their comfort in coming to work. Everything in my gut said that continuing to give him chances meant abandoning the people he was affecting.

He lost his job. I lost someone I'd genuinely hoped would turn things around, and I lost one of the most talented developers on the team. That wasn't a small business cost, but the women on our staff gained something more valuable. They gained proof that their reports mattered, that their safety wasn't secondary to someone else's technical abilities or potential.

The Decision No One Wanted

He had to go. Not because I wanted to give up on him. Not because I didn't believe people can change. Not because his technical skills weren't valuable; they absolutely were, and replacing that level of talent isn't easy, but because protecting the vulnerable isn't optional, and grace to one person can't come at the expense of everyone else's safety.

There's no feel-good ending here. I didn't enjoy it. I didn't feel victorious. I felt the weight of knowing that the same framework that extended grace in one situation demanded accountability in another.

Here's what happened: The women on my staff felt safe. Not because I told them they were safe, but because they'd watched me lead with integrity when it cost me something I valued. They knew I would actually protect them, not just talk about protecting them. They knew their reports would be taken seriously.

My reputation preceded the crisis. When other difficult situations arose, and they did, people came to me because they'd seen me make hard calls based on principle, not politics. They trusted that the framework would hold, even when the outcome was uncomfortable.

Why the Framework Works

This is the point that both Christian and secular leaders need to understand: A leadership framework that only works in easy situations isn't a framework. It's a preference.

The QA analyst story and this story aren't contradictions. They're the same framework applied to different contexts:

- **QA analyst:** Honest mistake, genuine remorse, no pattern of harm → Grace leads to restoration

- **This employee:** Pattern of harm, multiple chances, no meaningful change → Protection requires removal

One framework. Two outcomes. Both right.

The reason secular leaders should care: Teams that see you apply the same principles consistently, even when it costs you personally, develop trust that no team-building exercise can manufacture. They know the rules of the game. They know you'll extend grace when appropriate and enforce accountability when necessary. That predictability creates psychological safety.

The reason Christian leaders should care: This is what Biblical justice actually looks like. It's not just mercy, and it's not just judgment. It's applying the same principles to different situations and letting the context determine the outcome.

The Biblical Foundation

If you're looking for the Biblical grounding here, it's woven throughout Scripture:

Proverbs 31:8-9 "Open your mouth for the mute, for the rights of all who are destitute. Open your mouth, judge righteously, defend the rights of the poor and needy."

The women reporting harassment weren't literally mute, but they were vulnerable. They needed someone with authority to actually use it on their behalf.

1 Corinthians 5 shows Paul addressing a situation where someone's behavior was harming the community. His response wasn't endless chances. It was clear boundaries to protect the whole. He writes with deep sorrow, not vindictiveness, but he's unambiguous: protecting the community sometimes means removing the one causing harm.

Matthew 18:15-17 lays out Jesus' process for addressing sin and harm: private conversation, escalation with witnesses, involving the broader community, and ultimately treating the unrepentant person "as a Gentile and a tax collector" (which in that context meant recognizing they'd removed themselves from the community). Three chances. Clear process. Then protection of the whole takes precedence.

Notice the pattern: All three passages assume that grace and accountability come from the same root. You don't choose between being loving and being just. You love people enough to give them chances to change, and you love people enough to protect them when someone won't.

What This Means for You

If you're leading a team, you'll face this decision. Maybe not about harassment. Maybe about someone whose negativity is poisoning team culture, or someone whose incompetence is creating problems everyone else has to fix, or someone whose ethics are questionable enough to put others at risk.

Here's what I learned:

- **Don't wait for certainty.** You'll never have perfect information, but patterns tell you something. If you've given clear feedback and genuine chances, and the behavior persists, you have enough information.

- **Your discomfort is not the issue.** I didn't want to fire him. That discomfort was real, but my discomfort was less important than the safety of people I was responsible for protecting. Leaders get paid to be uncomfortable.

- **Grace and accountability aren't opposites.** The same framework that led me to give the junior analyst a second chance led me to remove this employee. I wasn't contradicting myself. I was being consistent. Different contexts, same principles.

- **Document everything.** Not because you're building a legal case (though that matters), but because clarity protects everyone. He knew exactly where he stood after each conversation. No surprises, no ambiguity.

- **Your reputation matters more than you think.** The reason women felt safe reporting to me wasn't because I promised to take them seriously. It was because they'd watched me make other hard calls based on principle. Your past decisions create the context for future trust.

The Weight of It

I won't pretend this was easy. I don't celebrate firing people. I don't enjoy being the person who has to tell someone their behavior has disqualified them from being part of the team.

I've learned this: The framework holds. Not because it makes hard decisions easy, but because it makes hard decisions clear. When you know what you value, when you've thought through how those values apply in complex situations, when you're willing to apply the same framework even when it costs you something, you can make the hard call and sleep at night. Not because you're always right, but because you're consistently principled.

In leadership, that's what builds cultures where people feel safe, where excellence matters, and where trust becomes the foundation for everything else you're trying to build.

Next: Chapter 8 will explore how this framework applies when you're not the decision-maker, when you're advising leadership on hard calls, or when you disagree with the decision authority has made. Consistency isn't just about what you do when you're in charge. It's about how you carry yourself when you're not.

Chapter Eight

When Integrity Costs You the Deal

S ome leadership decisions give you time to think. You can weigh options, consult advisors, sleep on it. This wasn't one of those decisions.

We walked into a sales meeting to pitch an addition to a product we were developing. It was genuinely groundbreaking technology, using AI to solve a major problem in the industry. What normally took multiple days could be done in minutes. Revolutionary, time-saving, exactly the kind of innovation that gets clients excited.

We knew what the application did. We knew what it didn't do. We understood its capabilities and its limitations. Clear boundaries, realistic expectations. Then the meeting started.

When the Pitch Goes Sideways

Minutes into the presentation, I could feel it. We weren't connecting. The client's body language shifted. Their questions went a different direction than we'd anticipated. We'd missed the mark on what they actually needed.

That's when our lead salesman started to pivot. He was senior, experienced, the guy who closed deals. I normally deferred to him in sales situations because that was his expertise, but as I sat there listening, I realized he wasn't just pivoting the pitch. He was making things up.

Features that didn't exist. A roadmap that was completely inaccurate. Promises we couldn't deliver. The kind of exaggerations that sound good in the moment but collapse under the weight of reality when you actually have to build what you've sold.

Every salesperson knows the temptation. The client wants something you don't have, and you can feel the deal slipping away. So you start stretching. "We're planning to add that." "That's definitely on our roadmap." "We can have that ready in your timeframe." Each statement technically defensible in isolation, but together they paint a picture that's fundamentally dishonest.

I had a choice, and I had maybe sixty seconds to make it.

The Real-Time Decision

- **Option one:**

Stay quiet. Let him finish the pitch. Try to walk it back later, maybe in a follow-up email where I could "clarify" what we meant. Preserve the relationship, keep the possibility of the deal alive, deal with the consequences down the road.

- **Option two:**

Speak up. Correct the misinformation in real time. Contradict my own salesman in front of the client. Almost certainly lose the deal, probably create tension with the sales team, definitely look like the difficult technical guy who doesn't understand how sales works.

Here's what was running through my head in those sixty seconds:

If I stay quiet, we might get a deal today, but when we can't deliver what he just promised, we'll lose them anyway. Plus our reputation. Plus any referrals they might have given. Plus my integrity, because I sat there and let lies stand when I knew the truth.

If I speak up, we'll probably lose the deal right now. I'll look like I'm undermining my own team. The salesman will be frustrated. The client will lose confidence that we even know what we're building. All the worst-case scenarios happen immediately instead of later.

Then there was the third thought, the one that almost got me: Could I somehow make this work? Could I build a team fast enough? Hire the right developers? Pull together the resources to turn his exaggerations into reality in their timeframe? My brain started doing the math. If I brought on two more developers, if we pushed the other project back, if we worked weekends, maybe...

Even as I was calculating, I knew the answer. No. Not in their timeframe. Not without sacrificing quality on everything else we'd committed to. Not without burning out the team. I could, maybe, deliver 70% of what he'd just promised, nine months late, at twice the cost. Which is just a slower, more expensive way to break their trust.

Here's the thing: Later was going to come. The truth was going to come out. The only question was whether it came out now, when we could still build something real, or later, when we'd already broken their trust and exhausted ourselves trying to deliver the impossible.

Speaking Truth to Power (And to Clients)

I interrupted. Not aggressively. Not in a way that completely undermined our sales rep, but clearly enough that everyone in the room knew I was correcting what had just been said. "Actually, that's not quite accurate. Here's what we can do..." and I laid out the truth. What our product actually did. What we were genuinely planning to build. What timeline was realistic. Where we had limitations.

The room got quiet. The kind of quiet where everyone's recalculating. The salesman's jaw tightened. The client looked confused, maybe a little uncomfortable with the obvious tension. I kept going. Not because I enjoyed it, but because stopping halfway through the truth is just a different kind of lie. "What I can promise you is this: We'll tell you the truth about what we can deliver, we'll build something that actually solves your problem, and we won't waste your time with features that only exist in a pitch deck." Then I stopped talking and waited to see if we still had a meeting.

What Truth Built

They became one of our largest clients. Not despite my honesty, because of it. Here's what happened: Once the air cleared and the awkwardness passed, we actually talked about their real needs. Not the imaginary product my salesman had invented, but what they genuinely needed solved and we found common ground. We built a product that actually met their needs, and it ended up serving others in the industry too. The relationship was built on realistic expectations and delivered promises, not inflated claims and inevitable disappointment.

Here's what matters most: The trust we built in that moment of discomfort became the foundation for everything else. When problems came up later, and they always do, they didn't assume we were hiding things or spinning the truth. They knew we'd shoot straight. That trust was worth more than any individual deal.

Months later, that client told me the reason they stayed was because they'd been burned before by vendors who promised everything and delivered half. Watching me correct my own salesman in real time told them something about how we'd handle problems down the road.

Why This Works (Even in Sales)

Secular leaders should care about this because the business case is overwhelming: Short-term wins built on exaggeration create long-term losses. Clients expect to be sold to. They expect some optimism, some vision-casting, some "best case scenario" thinking. But there's a line between optimism and dishonesty, and crossing it costs you more than the deal you're trying to save.

When you build relationships on truth:

- Problems become conversations, not betrayals

- Clients give you more time to solve things because they trust your assessment

- Referrals increase because people know you won't embarrass them

- Your reputation precedes you in ways that close future deals

When you build relationships on exaggeration:

- Every problem becomes evidence you're a liar

- Clients assume the worst because they don't trust your spin

- Referrals dry up because people won't risk their own reputation

- Your reputation precedes you in ways that kill future deals

It's not idealism. It's just math. Trust compounds. Distrust compounds faster. Christian leaders should care about this because it's not just about business outcomes. It's about who you're becoming in the process. Every time you let a lie stand, you train yourself to value the deal more than the truth. Every time you prioritize closing over honesty, you reshape your character in ways that leak into everything else you lead.

You can't compartmentalize integrity. You can't be one kind of leader in sales meetings and a different kind of leader everywhere else. Your team is watching. Your character is forming. The person you become in pressure moments is the person you're becoming.

The Biblical Foundation

If you're looking for the Biblical grounding, it's not subtle:

> **Proverbs 12:22** "Lying lips are an abomination to the Lord, but those who act faithfully are his delight."

Not "lying is suboptimal" or "dishonesty has trade-offs." Abomination. God's not neutral on this. Faithfulness in how you represent truth isn't optional for leaders who claim to follow him.

Proverbs 11:3 "The integrity of the upright guides them, but the crookedness of the treacherous destroys them."

Notice the long-term framing. Integrity guides. Crookedness destroys. Not immediately, but inevitably. The deals you get through dishonesty carry the seeds of their own destruction.

Proverbs 21:6 "The getting of treasures by a lying tongue is a fleeting vapor and a snare of death."

The verse describes exactly what my salesman was attempting, getting a deal through exaggeration, and it predicts the outcome: fleeting (won't last) and a snare (will trap you). The deal you gain through dishonesty carries the seeds of its own destruction.

Colossians 3:9 "Do not lie to one another, seeing that you have put off the old self with its practices."

For Christian leaders, lying isn't just a tactic you avoid because it's risky. It's a practice you've left behind because it belongs to a way of living you've rejected. This isn't just religious preference. This is how reality works. Truth builds. Lies destroy. Every time. Eventually.

What This Means for You

You're going to face this decision. Maybe not in a sales meeting. Maybe in a job interview where exaggerating your experience could get you the role. Maybe in a client meeting where downplaying a problem could buy you time. Maybe in a board presentation where spinning the numbers could save your project.

Here's what I learned:

- **The cost is immediate. The payoff is cumulative.** Speaking truth in that meeting felt terrible. Watching the deal nearly die was painful. But every interaction after that was built on a foundation that made everything else easier. You pay the cost of honesty once. You pay the cost of dishonesty forever.

- **Your reputation is your most valuable asset.** That salesman could close deals, but if clients can't trust what comes out of his mouth, every deal requires more effort, more convincing, more energy spent overcoming skepticism. When people know you tell the truth even when it costs you, your words carry weight that no pitch deck can manufacture.

- **Silence is agreement.** I could have stayed quiet and told myself I didn't lie. But sitting there while someone else misrepresents reality on your behalf is just outsourcing your dishonesty. If you're in the room and you know the truth, you own what gets said.

- **The team is watching.** After that meeting, everyone knew where I stood. Future sales conversations had a different tone because the salespeople knew I wouldn't let exaggerations stand. That wasn't comfortable for them initially, but it forced us to get better at selling what we actually had and that made us better at building what people actually needed.

- **Trust is binary.** Clients don't trust you 80% or give you partial credibility. Either they believe what you say, or they don't. Once dishonesty enters the relationship, everything else you say gets filtered through that lens. You can't rebuild trust by being honest most of the time.

The Weight of Speaking Up

I won't pretend this was comfortable. Contradicting your own sales-man in front of a client feels terrible. The tension in the room was real. The risk was real. Part of me wanted to stay quiet, let him finish, deal with it later. I've learned this: The discomfort of speaking truth in the moment is nothing compared to the slow erosion of living with lies. The first costs you a deal. The second costs you your integrity.

When you know the truth, when you have the authority to speak, when staying silent means letting dishonesty stand, you have a re-sponsibility. Not just to the client, though that matters. Not just to your company, though that matters too, but to yourself, to the kind of leader you're becoming in those pressure moments.

The framework held. Not because it made the decision easy, but because it made the decision clear. Short-term loss, long-term gain. Immediate discomfort, cumulative trust. The deal I risked losing by telling the truth became the relationship I couldn't have built with lies.

In leadership, that's what integrity actually means. Not refusing to compromise when it's convenient, but choosing truth when it costs you something you want.

Next: Chapter 9 will explore what happens when you fail to apply the framework, when you compromise under pressure, and how to recover when you've made the wrong call. Consistency isn't about being perfect. It's about what you do after you fall short.

Chapter Nine

What Happens When You Violate the Framework

I 've spent the last few chapters showing you stories where the framework held. Where choosing integrity over convenience led to better outcomes. Where truth built trust and trust built business. Now let me show you what happens when you ignore it.

The $350,000 Error

A client was mis-billed nearly 1,000 hours on a project. Our hourly rate was $350/hour. You do the math. This wasn't a rounding error or a minor discrepancy. This was a $350,000 accounting mistake, in our favor.

Neither company realized it at the time. The invoice went out. They paid it. Project closed. Everyone moved on. The following month, our accounting team discovered the error during their routine reconciliation. They brought it to leadership's attention. The client clearly wasn't going to catch it on their own. Their accounting had moved on. The project was in the past. We had a decision to make.

The Pressure to Keep Quiet

Our CFO at the time had a strong opinion: Don't report it. Just keep the money and move forward like nothing happened. His argument was compelling, at least on the surface. If we refunded $350,000, we'd have to make up that revenue somehow. That meant layoffs. Specifically, he calculated we'd need to lay off two people on my team to cover the shortfall.

Two people I knew. Two people who trusted me to look out for them. Two people with families, mortgages, lives built around the assumption they had stable jobs. I could save those jobs by doing nothing. Just not mentioning an error that nobody else had caught.

The CFO framed it as a leadership decision. "You care about your team, right? You want to protect their jobs? Then this is what protecting them looks like." I knew it was wrong. Internally, everything in me said this violated the framework. Truth matters. Integrity matters. You can't build lasting relationships on hidden errors, even accidental ones. Even ones that benefit you. I also knew those two people on my team. I'd hired them. I'd invested in them, and now I had the power to protect their jobs by simply staying quiet about something that was ancient history anyway.

So I tried to stand up for the right thing. Initially. I pushed back against the CFO. I made the case for transparency, for telling the client, for correcting the error. But he kept coming back to the same argument: "You're going to destroy two people's livelihoods over an accounting error nobody else even knows about?"

Then the CEO weighed in on the CFO's side. That's when I caved.

The Rationalization

Here's how I justified it to myself:

- *This isn't like lying in a sales meeting. That was proactive dishonesty. This is just... not volunteering information. There's a difference, right?*

- *The client had every opportunity to catch this themselves. If they couldn't manage their own accounting, why should we bail them out?*

- *I'm protecting my team. That's what good leaders do. Sometimes you have to make hard calls to keep people employed.*

- *It was an honest mistake on both sides. We didn't intentionally overbill them. So correcting it is more about optics than ethics.*

- *Time has passed. Bringing it up now would just create awkwardness and complications for everyone. Moving forward is cleaner.*

Every one of those rationalizations felt plausible at the time. I could construct a narrative where I wasn't the bad guy. I was the pragmatic leader making a tough call to protect his people. I was being realistic about business. I was avoiding unnecessary drama. I told myself I was doing this for good reasons, and that made it feel less wrong.

The Three Months

I wish I could tell you I completely forgot about it. That I rationalized it so successfully that it never crossed my mind again, but that's not how conscience works. Most days, I didn't think about it. We moved on to other projects, other clients, other challenges. Life continued, but then something would trigger the memory.

A conversation with that client would feel slightly off. Not because they suspected anything, but because I knew something they didn't. Every interaction carried a weight they couldn't see. An invoice would cross my desk and I'd remember. The accounting team would close another month and I'd think about what we were hiding in the books.

Conversations about integrity in leadership meetings felt hollow. I'd say the right things, but I knew I hadn't lived them. I never lost sleep over it. I never had some crisis of conscience that drove me to confess. I just carried this low-grade discomfort that I got good at pushing down. The weight was there, but I'd gotten used to carrying it.

Until three months later, when I didn't have to carry it anymore, because they found it.

When Truth Catches Up

Their accounting team caught the error during their semi-annual audit. They sent us a polite but firm email asking about the discrepancy. They'd done their homework. They had the receipts. The timeline. The comparison to project scope. They knew.

We had to refund the money. All of it. Just like we would have three months earlier when we first discovered it. Except now, we had to do it while also explaining why we hadn't mentioned it when our accounting team found it. We couldn't explain it. At least, not in any way that didn't make us look either incompetent or dishonest.

The CFO's "job protection" argument evaporated instantly. We still had to make up the revenue. The two people on my team? We still faced the same financial pressure. I hadn't protected anyone by staying quiet. I'd just delayed the inevitable while destroying something far more valuable: trust.

We lost them as a client. Not immediately, not dramatically. They finished their existing contracts with us. But the referrals stopped. The new project conversations dried up. The relationship went from partnership to transaction, and eventually, to nothing at all.

Everything I'd been trying to protect by keeping quiet got destroyed anyway. The jobs, the revenue, the client relationship, all of it. Plus, I lost something I couldn't get back: my own integrity in that situation, and their trust in us as a company.

Why This Story Matters

I could have left this story out. You'd never have known. The previous chapters show me making the right calls, building trust, leading with integrity. I could have maintained that image, but that would be another kind of dishonesty.

I'm not telling you about a leadership framework I've mastered. I'm telling you about principles that work whether I follow them or not. Sometimes, I don't follow them. Sometimes the pressure gets to me. Sometimes I convince myself that my motives justify my methods. Sometimes I fail. When I fail, the framework still proves itself. Not by making things better, but by showing me exactly what gets destroyed when you violate it.

Here's what I learned from getting it wrong:

- **"Good" motives don't justify wrong actions.** I genuinely wanted to protect jobs. That wasn't manipulation or spin. That was a real concern, but wanting to do good doesn't make a dishonest action honest. Intent doesn't change the nature of the choice.

- **The thing you try to protect through dishonesty gets destroyed regardless.** I kept the money to save jobs and preserve the client relationship. I lost both. Not because confessing would have guaranteed keeping them, but because the cover-up poisoned everything once the truth came out. **The truth always comes out.**

- **Confession up front would have preserved the relationship.** If we'd caught the error and immediately reported it, would it have been uncomfortable? Absolutely. Would they have been frustrated? Probably. They'd have seen integrity under pressure. Instead, they saw us hide a mistake for three months. One of those builds trust. The other destroys it.

- **The cover-up always costs more than the truth.** Three months of carrying that weight, of compromised interactions, of leadership conversations that felt hollow because I knew I'd failed my own standards. Then the damage when they discovered it. Then the loss of the relationship. All of that cost more than the discomfort of being honest when we first found the error.

- **Rationalization is your enemy.** The most dangerous moment wasn't when the CFO pressured me. It was when I started agreeing with him. When I started constructing narratives where keeping the money was actually the responsible thing to do. Once you start believing your own rationalizations, you've lost the internal compass that tells you when you're going the wrong direction.

The Biblical Warning

Scripture isn't subtle about this:

> **Proverbs 28:13** "Whoever conceals his transgressions will not prosper, but he who confesses and forsakes them will obtain mercy."

Notice the structure. Concealing leads to failure. Confessing leads to mercy. This isn't a suggestion. This is how reality works. I concealed the transgression. I didn't prosper. The relationship failed, the trust evaporated, everything I tried to protect fell apart. The proverb predicted it perfectly.

> **Numbers 32:23** "Be sure your sin will find you out."

Not "might find you out" or "could find you out." Will. Inevitability. You can rationalize, justify, bury, or ignore. Doesn't matter. Truth catches up. Three months. That's how long it took in my case. Sometimes it's longer. Sometimes it's shorter. But it's never "never."

James 1:22 "But be doers of the word, and not hearers only, deceiving yourselves."

That's what rationalization is. Self-deception. I knew what the right thing was. I'd taught it to my team. I'd applied it in other situations, but in this moment, I heard the truth and didn't do it and the person I deceived most effectively wasn't the client. It was myself.

What This Means for You

You're going to face pressure to compromise. Maybe not about a billing error. Maybe about covering for someone else's mistake. Maybe about staying quiet when you should speak up. Maybe about exaggerating results to save a project. Maybe about hiding a problem until you can fix it so no one has to know.

You're going to be tempted to construct narratives where compromise is actually wisdom. Where dishonesty is really just pragmatism. Where the ends justify the means because your motives are good.

Here's what I wish I'd known then:

- **The framework doesn't fail. You do.** The principles don't stop working because you ignore them. They just prove themselves through negative example. When I followed the framework in the sales meeting, it built trust. When I violated it with the billing error, it destroyed trust. Same principles, different outcomes based on my choices.

- **The pressure you feel is real, but it's lying to you.** The CFO's argument felt compelling because the stakes were real. Jobs mattered. Revenue mattered. The pressure was telling me that dishonesty would solve the problem. It didn't. It never does. Pressure amplifies the consequences of your decision, but it doesn't change which decision is right.

- **You don't get to keep what you gain dishonestly.** Even when nobody catches it, you've lost something. Your integrity. Your peace. Your internal alignment between what you believe and how you act, and when they do catch it, and they will, you lose everything else too.

- **The way back starts with admission.** I'm not telling you this story because I've moved past it or because enough time has passed that it doesn't matter. I'm telling you because owning your failures is how you rebuild integrity. Not pretending they didn't happen. Not minimizing them. Not explaining them away. Just admitting: I knew better. I did it anyway. It cost me.

- **Your framework is only as good as your worst moment.** Everyone can lead with integrity when it's easy. The question is what you do when following your principles costs you something you desperately want to keep. That's where you find out whether you have a framework or just a preference.

The Hard Truth

I didn't write this book because I've figured it all out. I wrote it because I've learned, often painfully, that these principles hold whether you follow them or not. When I applied the framework with the junior analyst, grace led to loyalty. When I applied it with the inappropriate employee, protection created safety. When I applied it in the sales meeting, truth built partnership.

When I violated the framework with the billing error, dishonesty destroyed everything I tried to protect. Same principles. Different choices. Predictable outcomes. The framework works. Even when I don't. Especially when I don't.

Next: Part 3 begins with how to implement this framework at your organization. How to hire for character, how to model humility, and how small, every day mundane, decisions build your reputation, not the crisis moments.

Part 3

Big decisions reveal your character. Small decisions build it.

You can navigate a crisis with integrity, extend grace under pressure, protect vulnerable people when it costs you, and still fail at leadership if you don't pay attention to the daily behaviors nobody notices. The way you hire. The way you make decisions with your team. The way you show up when nothing dramatic is happening. The pattern, over time, that teaches people what to expect from you.

This section is about the unglamorous work of leadership. Not the production outages at 2 AM or the harassment reports that force decisive action. The Tuesday morning meetings where you either invite challenge or shut it down. The hiring interviews where you either test for character or settle for credentials. The thousand small choices that either align with your values or reveal you don't actually hold them.

Culture isn't built in crisis. Crisis reveals the culture you've already built through those small, daily, unnoticed decisions. The team that trusts you during a catastrophe learned to trust you during normal days when you kept your word, admitted your mistakes, and treated people with dignity even when no one was watching.

This is where principles become patterns. Where framework becomes culture. Where the leader you are when nothing's at stake shapes the leader you'll be when everything is.

Let me show you how the small things compound into something that lasts.

Chapter Ten

Hiring for Character

The Interview That Tests What Matters

Most professional interviews follow a predictable pattern: technical assessments, case studies, behavioral scenarios. You're testing competence. Can they analyze a balance sheet? Do they understand regulatory compliance? Can they manage complex projects? Have they worked in your industry?

I test for something different. Not because competence doesn't matter. It absolutely does, but because I've learned the hard way that brilliant jerks destroy more value than they create. I've watched high-credentialed professionals derail projects because they couldn't accept feedback. I've seen talented people poison team culture because they needed to be the smartest person in every conversation.

Competence is the baseline. Character is the multiplier. You can test for it in an interview if you know what to look for, or more precisely: if you create the conditions where character reveals itself under pressure.

The Biblical Foundation

Before I explain the process, let me show you why it works. The book of Proverbs, three thousand years of collected wisdom, has a consistent thread running through it about ego and teachability:

> **Proverbs 12:15** "The way of a fool is right in his own eyes, but a wise man listens to advice."

> **Proverbs 26:12** "Do you see a man who is wise in his own eyes? There is more hope for a fool than for him."

Notice what these passages are testing: **not intelligence, but teachability.** The person who's "wise in his own eyes" is beyond hope, not because they lack brains, but because they've closed themselves off to input. They can't be sharpened because they don't think they need sharpening. There's another dimension Scripture tests that most people miss: how you handle being right.

Paul writes to the Philippians:

> **Philippians 2:3** "Do nothing from selfish ambition or conceit, but in humility count others more significant than yourselves."

In his qualifications for church leadership, he lists:

1 Timothy 3:3 "not violent but gentle, not quarrelsome."

You see this tested throughout Jesus' ministry. Watch how he treats people when he has every advantage:

- The woman caught in adultery (John 8): He's sinless; she's guilty. He has the moral high ground. What does he do? Protects her from the crowd, then speaks truth gently: "Go and sin no more."

- The Samaritan woman at the well (John 4): He knows her entire history, all her failures, all her shame. He could humiliate her. Instead, he offers living water and reveals himself as Messiah.

- Peter after the denial (John 21): Jesus had predicted Peter would deny him. Peter did exactly that. Jesus could rub it in. Instead, he restores him: "Feed my sheep."

Here's the pattern: When Jesus had the advantage, when he was obviously right and others were obviously wrong, he didn't gloat. He didn't condescend. He corrected with truth, but he guided with gentleness. Most interviews test whether someone can handle being challenged. That's important.

I test something most people miss: How do they handle being right? That's when ego reveals itself most clearly.

The Real Test: An Ego Detection System

Here's what I actually do in a 30-60 minute interview. I bring the candidate in for a technical discussion. We talk through their experience, their approach to problems, their technical philosophy. Normal interview stuff for the first portion.

Then I present a real-world scenario, usually something close to an actual challenge we're facing. Maybe it's about architecting a data pipeline, or handling API rate limits, or designing a notification system. Something meaty enough to have multiple valid approaches.

I ask them: "How would you solve this?"

They propose their solution. They walk me through their reasoning. So far, so standard. Then I propose a different approach. Sometimes it's worse than theirs. Sometimes it's better. Sometimes it's just different. Honestly? The technical quality of the ideas doesn't matter. What matters is what happens next. Now I'm watching for ego.

What I'm Actually Watching For

Test #1: How Do They React When Challenged?

When I push back on their solution or propose a different approach, I'm watching:

- **Facial expressions:** Do they tense up? Do their eyes narrow? Does their body language shift to defensive?

- **Tone:** Does their voice get harder? More insistent? Do they start talking faster, like they need to convince me before I interrupt again?

- **What they say:** Do they get defensive and double down on a truly terrible idea? Do they make excuses for why their approach is still better even when it clearly has flaws? Or do they stay open, ask questions, genuinely consider the alternative?

- **How they make me feel:** Do they dismiss my suggestion in a way that makes me feel stupid for bringing it up? Or do they engage with it respectfully, even if they ultimately disagree?

The person who gets combative, inflexible, defensive? That's ego, and ego under the low-pressure environment of an interview becomes toxicity under the high-pressure environment of a production crisis. There's a second test that's even more revealing.

Test #2: How Do They React When They're Right?

This is the one most interviewers miss. Sometimes a candidate proposes a solution that's genuinely better than what I had in mind, or I'll deliberately propose something that has an obvious flaw, and they'll catch it. When that happens, I do something most CTOs don't: I admit it out loud.

"You know what? You're right. I'm absolutely wrong on that. Good catch."

Then I watch.

- **Facial expressions:** Do they smile smugly? Do they look pleased with themselves for catching the CTO's mistake, or do they stay serious and focused on solving the problem?

- **Tone:** Do they get jovial and joke about it? Do they laugh like they just won something, or do they stay professional and guide the conversation forward?

- **What they say:** Do they explain why my idea won't work

in a way that makes me feel dumb, or do they gently correct
and guide me to why their solution is better, pointing out the
specific flaw without condescension?

- **How they make me feel:** Do I feel talked down to, like I'm
  being educated by someone who's enjoying their superiority,
  or do I feel like we're collaborating to find the best answer?

This is where character reveals itself most clearly. Anyone can be
gracious when they're wrong. That's socially expected. Being gracious
when you're right, when you've just proven you're smarter than the
person across from you who has authority and power, that takes genuine humility.

The person who gloats, even subtly? The person who makes me
feel dumb for missing something obvious? That's ego, and that ego
will poison every code review, every architectural decision, every team
meeting they're part of. The person who stays humble in victory? Who
corrects gently, explains clearly, and moves forward without rubbing
it in?

That's the person I hire.

Why This Works: Testing Character Under Pressure in Both Directions

This isn't about the ideas. I don't actually care whether their solution
is better or worse than mine. I'm not testing technical judgment; I can
teach that.

I'm testing ego under pressure.

I test it in both directions:

- **When they're challenged:** Do they stay open or get defensive?

- **When they're right:** Do they stay gracious or gloat?

Most people can manage one or the other. The rare person who can handle both, who can receive challenge with humility AND deliver correction with grace, that's the character foundation I can build on.

This works equally well for junior developers and senior architects. A 22-year-old can have just as much ego as a 65-year-old. The job level doesn't matter. The character does.

The Biblical Foundation: Teachability + Grace Under Advantage

This two-directional test maps directly to Scripture:

Test #1: Can You Receive Correction?

> **Proverbs 12:15** "The way of a fool is right in his own eyes, but a wise man listens to advice."

> **Proverbs 12:1** "Whoever loves discipline loves knowledge, but he who hates reproof is stupid."

Paul models this himself:

> **Philippians 3:12** "Not that I have already obtained
> this or am already perfect, but I press on to make it my
> own."

The wise person knows they might be wrong. They expect to have blind spots. They invite challenge because they care more about truth than being right.

Test #2: How Do You Treat People When You Have the Advantage?

> **Philippians 2:3** "Do nothing from selfish ambition
> or conceit, but in humility count others more signifi-
> cant than yourselves."

> **Ephesians 4:29** "Let no corrupting talk come out of
> your mouths, but only such as is good for building up,
> as fits the occasion, that it may give grace to those who
> hear."

> **Proverbs 15:1** "A soft answer turns away wrath, but
> a harsh word stirs up anger."

Jesus demonstrated this pattern constantly. When he corrected people, he did it with truth but also with gentleness, especially with those who were genuinely seeking. The harsh corrections were reserved for the proud and hypocritical who should have known better.

The person who passes both tests demonstrates teachability (test #1) and gracious strength (test #2). That's the character combination that builds healthy teams.

Making Yourself Vulnerable: The Strategic Move

Here's why I explicitly admit when I'm wrong in an interview:

I'm modeling the culture they're walking into. If I say I value humility and collaboration, but I can't admit when a candidate is right and I'm wrong, then I'm just another leader who talks about values but doesn't live them. When I say "You're right, I missed that, good catch," and I mean it, I'm doing three things:

1. **Testing their character:** How do they handle victory?
2. **Modeling the culture:** This is how we treat each other here
3. **Building trust:** If I can admit I'm wrong in an interview, they know I'll do it after they're hired

This vulnerability is strategic. It creates the conditions where ego reveals itself. It filters for people who'll thrive in a culture where the best idea wins, not the loudest voice or the highest title.

The Success Rate: Better Than the Alternative

I need to be honest: this process isn't foolproof. About 80% of my hires turn out well. About 20% fool me; they pass the interview, but once they're hired, the ego I was trying to detect shows up anyway. Sometimes in retrospect there were subtle red flags I missed. Sometimes they're just really good actors for 60 minutes.

Interviews are artificial. You're trying to assess someone's character in a controlled, low-stakes environment, then predict how they'll behave in real pressure situations. It's inherently limited. 80% is still way better than hiring based on credentials and technical skills alone, and even when I miss, I learn. I go back and review what I might have caught. I refine what I'm watching for. I get slightly better at detecting the tells.

The point isn't perfection. The point is intentionality. Most organizations don't test for character at all. This at least creates the conditions where character has a chance to reveal itself.

What Gentle Correction Actually Looks Like

Let me give you examples of what I'm listening for when someone corrects my deliberately flawed idea:

Bad correction (ego showing):

- "Yeah, that won't work because [explains in a way that makes it obvious I should have known this]"

- "I actually thought about that approach, but it's got some pretty serious problems"

- [Laughs] "I mean, you could do that, but..."

- [Talks for five minutes explaining why I'm wrong, clearly enjoying the teaching moment]

Good correction (humble strength):

- "I think that might run into issues in our environment. Would it handle [specific constraint]?"

- "That's an interesting approach. I'm concerned about [specific problem]. How would that work?"

- "I see what you're going for. One thing we'd need to consider is [flaw], which might make [candidate's approach] more reliable"

- "Good question. The main issue I see is [flaw]. If we could solve that, your approach might work, but I think [alternative] might be simpler."

You see the difference? The first set makes me feel dumb. The second set treats me like a peer we're solving a problem together, even while pointing out the flaw in my thinking. That's the character I'm hiring for.

The Four Qualities This Reveals

When someone passes both tests, handles challenge with humility AND handles being right with grace, they're demonstrating four essential character traits:

1. Openness to Challenge

Proverbs 27:17 "Iron sharpens iron, and one man sharpens another."

In practice: This is the person who'll tell you in a planning meeting that the timeline doesn't work. Who'll push back when promises are made they can't keep. Who'll raise concerns about technical debt before it becomes a crisis.

2. Humility Under Correction

> **Proverbs 26:12** "Do you see a man who is wise in his own eyes? There is more hope for a fool than for him."

In practice: This is the person who'll revise their approach after code review feedback. Who'll learn from junior developers when they spot something. Who'll change direction when new information emerges.

3. Gracious Strength

> **Philippians 2:3** "Do nothing from selfish ambition or conceit, but in humility count others more significant than yourselves."

In practice: This is the person who corrects without condescension. Who challenges without attacking. Who can be right without needing you to feel wrong.

4. Truth Over Ego

Proverbs 23:23 "Buy truth, and do not sell it; buy wisdom, instruction, and understanding."

In practice: This is the person who values truth enough to "buy" it (pursue it at cost to ego). Who cares more about finding the right answer than being the one who had it. Who prioritizes team success over personal recognition. Who sees collaboration as abundance, not competition.

Building the Culture You Want

This interview process isn't just about filtering out difficult people. It's about building a specific kind of culture. I want a team that challenges me. Not because I enjoy conflict, but because I'm wrong all the time and I need people who'll tell me. If I hire people who won't challenge me, I'm stuck with the limitations of my own thinking. Every decision runs through my assumptions, my blind spots, my biases. The team becomes an echo chamber.

If I hire people who have both the courage to say "I think you're missing something" AND the humility to hear it back, now we're building something better than any of us could create individually. The interview process filters for this. The candidate who can challenge me respectfully is the person who'll make the team better. The candidate who can receive challenge gracefully is the person who'll make themselves better. Both qualities matter. Both are testable. Both are rooted in Biblical wisdom about character.

The Secular Translation: Why This Works Everywhere

If you're reading this as a non-Christian leader wondering if this is just "spiritual hiring," let me be direct: this works because it's true, not because it's religious. Proverbs isn't "faith-based advice"; it's observed reality. These aren't arbitrary rules; they're descriptions of how wisdom actually functions in the world.

Humble people do learn faster. Teachable people do grow more. People who can be gracious when they're right do build stronger teams. People who can handle being wrong do contribute more value over time. You don't need to believe in the Bible to see that these character traits produce better outcomes.

The question is: Are you testing for them?

Most organizations say they value "collaboration" and "growth mindset" and "respectful challenge." Then they hire based on credentials and technical performance and never actually assess whether candidates have those qualities. This interview process tests what you say you value. It creates controlled pressure, not high stakes, but enough friction to see how someone's character responds and character under low pressure predicts character under high pressure.

The Connection to the Framework

Remember the four-part leadership framework:

1. **Humility** - "Who am I to judge? What am I missing?"

2. **Whole Counsel** - "What's the complete human and business impact?"

3. **Restoration or Protection** - "Can this be fixed or does someone need defending?"

4. **Moral Intuition** - "Does this feel right based on principles,

not politics?"

This hiring process directly tests for people who'll operate within that framework.

- **Humility:** Do they assume they might be wrong? Can they consider alternative perspectives? Can they admit when someone else is right?

- **Whole Counsel:** Do they think through implications? Do they ask clarifying questions? Do they consider how their correction makes others feel?

- **Restoration:** When challenged, do they get defensive (self-protection) or curious (seeking better understanding)?

- **Moral Intuition:** Do they prioritize truth over ego? Do they care more about the right answer than being right?

You're not just hiring skills. You're hiring people who'll reinforce the culture you're building, one where humility, context, restoration, and principle matter more than politics, ego, and self-protection.

My Rough Edge

I need to be honest about something. This process works. I stand by it. About 80% of the time, it helps me hire people who fit the culture and contribute real value, but I still have favorites. Not egregiously. I think I hide it pretty well, but everyone has people they click with more naturally, and I'm no exception.

The question I have to keep asking myself: Are my favorites based on character and competence, or just people who make me comfortable?

There's a difference between:

- "I trust this person because they've consistently demonstrated good judgment under pressure"

- "I like this person because we communicate in similar ways and they don't challenge me as much"

The first is legitimate. The second is bias. The interview process helps with this. It gives me objective data about character traits that matter, but I still have to audit myself. Am I giving opportunities to people who've earned them through demonstrated character or am I gravitating toward people who make my life easier?

> **Proverbs 21:2** "Every way of a man is right in his own eyes, but the LORD weighs the heart."

Translation: You can justify your hiring and promotion decisions all day long, but are you actually measuring what matters, or just what makes you comfortable? I'm still learning to answer that honestly.

The Practical Takeaway

If you take one thing from this chapter, take this:
You can teach skills. You cannot teach character under pressure.
Test for teachability. Test for humility. Test for how people handle being right and being wrong. Create the conditions in your interview where ego has a chance to reveal itself. Then watch carefully. The person who can say "I think you're wrong" AND "You're right, I missed that" in the same conversation? That's the person you build teams with.

The person who needs to win more than they need to find truth? That's the person who destroys teams, no matter how brilliant they are. Credentials tell you what someone's learned. Character tells you what they'll do when everything goes wrong at 2 AM and nobdy's watching. Hire accordingly.

Reflection Questons:

1. Think about your last hiring process. What did you actually test for? Competence? Credentials? Culture fit? Character under pressure?

2. When was the last time someone on your team corrected you? How did they do it? How did it make you feel? What does that tell you about the culture you've   built?

3. Who are your favorites on your team? Are they people who've earned trust through demonstrated character, or people who just make your life easier?

4. If you implemented this two-directional ego test in your next interview, what would you learn about yourself based on how you respond when candidates are right and you're wrong?

Chapter Eleven

Best Answer Wins

The Meeting Where I Changed My Mind

We're forty minutes into an architecture review. I've been pushing a particular approach to our API redesign for weeks. I've thought it through, documented it, made my case. I'm confident it's the right call.

Then a junior developer, maybe six months on the team, raises his hand.

"I think we're missing something," he says.

He walks through a scenario I hadn't considered. An edge case that exposes a fundamental flaw in my approach. The room goes quiet. Everyone's looking at me. I could defend my position. Find holes in his logic. Pull rank. Remind everyone who's been doing this for 18 years and who's been doing it for six months, or I could admit the obvious.

"You're right," I say. "That breaks my whole approach. We need to rethink this."

The meeting shifts. We rebuild the architecture around his insight. Three months later, that decision saves us from a production disaster.

This is what "best answer wins" looks like in practice, and it only works if you're willing to lose.

The Biblical Foundation

Before I explain how this works, let me show you why it works. Scripture is relentlessly clear about seeking counsel:

> **Proverbs 15:22** "Without counsel plans fail, but with many advisers they succeed."

> **Proverbs 11:14** "Where there is no guidance, a people falls, but in an abundance of counselors there is safety."

> **Proverbs 12:15** "The way of a fool is right in his own eyes, but a wise man listens to advice."

Notice the pattern. Wisdom isn't about having all the answers. It's about recognizing you don't and seeking input from others who might see what you're missing, but here's where it gets tricky. Proverbs also says this:

> **Proverbs 16:7** "When a man's ways please the LORD, he makes even his enemies to be at peace with him."

And this:

> **Proverbs 26:12** "Do you see a man who is wise in his
> own eyes? There is more hope for a fool than for him."

Scripture balances seeking counsel with the danger of being "wise
in your own eyes." The problem isn't authority itself. The problem is
authority that refuses input because it thinks it already knows. Leaders
who don't seek counsel make worse decisions, but leaders who can't
make decisions after seeking counsel aren't leading at all. The question
is: how do you balance the two?

The Approach: How "Best Answer Wins" Actually Works

Here's my process for making decisions:

1. Seek Input Before Deciding

I don't call a meeting to announce what I've decided. I call a meeting
to explore the problem together.

This means:

- **Framing the problem, not the solution.** "We need to redesign the API" not "Here's how we're redesigning the API."

- **Inviting alternatives.** "What am I missing? What would
  you do?"

- **Listening more than talking.** The goal is to hear perspectives I haven't considered.

The junior developer who caught my flaw? He only spoke up because the culture allowed it. If I'd opened the meeting with "here's what we're doing," he would have stayed quiet and we would have shipped a broken architecture.

2. Best Idea Wins, Regardless of Source

Title doesn't determine truth. The CTO can be wrong. The junior developer can be right.

This requires:

- **Separating ego from evaluation.** Can you admit when someone else's idea is better?

- **Evaluating on merit, not rank.** Does the logic hold? Does it solve the problem?

- **Crediting the source.** "As [name] pointed out..." not claiming their insight as yours.

This is where most leaders fail. They SAY they want input, but they only accept input that confirms what they already believed. That's not collaboration. That's theater.

3. When the Room Is Split, I Make the Call

This isn't leadership by committee. When there's genuine disagreement and no clear consensus, someone has to decide. That someone is me because that's what leadership is.

Here's the key: **I always explain why.**

Not "because I'm the boss." Not "because I said so." But "here's the reasoning: [specific explanation of why option A over option B]."

This does two things:

- **It forces me to articulate my logic.** Sometimes in explaining the decision, I realize it doesn't hold up. Better to catch that in the meeting than in production.

- **It shows the team I'm making a reasoned call, not an arbitrary one.** Even if they disagree, they can see the thought process.

4. I Reserve the Right to Overrule Myself

Sometimes I make the call, and then new information emerges that changes the picture.

When that happens, I say so.

"I made the call last week to go with option A. Based on what we've learned since then, I think option B is actually better. Here's why."

This isn't weakness. This is what Proverbs describes: **"The wise man listens to advice."** If I'm so committed to being right that I can't change my mind when the facts change, I'm not leading. I'm just protecting my ego.

The Balance: Not Committee, Not Autocracy

Here's what this is NOT:

It's not leadership by committee. I'm not taking a vote. I'm not letting the team decide by consensus every time. That creates paralysis, and no one's accountable.

It's not autocracy either. I'm not making unilateral decisions without input, then expecting blind obedience.

It's stewardship of authority with transparency.

God gives leaders authority. That authority comes with responsibility to lead well. Leading well means seeking counsel, making reasoned decisions, and being willing to admit when you're wrong. Think about how Moses led. When his father-in-law Jethro visited and saw Moses judging every dispute himself, Jethro gave him counsel:

> Exodus 18:17-18 "What you are doing is not good. You and the people with you will certainly wear yourselves out, for the thing is too heavy for you. You are not able to do it alone."

Moses could have pulled rank. "I'm the one who talked to God on the mountain. Who are you to tell me how to lead?"

He didn't.

Exodus 18:24 Moses listened.

He restructured the entire judicial system based on his father-in-law's advice because the advice was good, and Moses was secure enough to receive it. That's the model. Seek counsel. Make the call. Be willing to change when you're wrong.

The Biblical Foundation: Leaders Need Counsel AND Conviction

This tension exists throughout Scripture. King Solomon, considered the wisest man who ever lived, surrounded himself with counselors:

Proverbs 11:14 "In an abundance of counselors there is safety."

But Solomon also made the final call. When two women claimed the same baby, Solomon proposed cutting the baby in half. The counselors didn't vote. Solomon made a decisive judgment based on his insight into human nature. (1 Kings 3:16-28)

King Rehoboam, Solomon's son, failed at this balance. When he became king, the people asked him to lighten the heavy burdens Solomon had placed on them. Rehoboam sought counsel from two groups:

The elders who had served his father advised:

1 Kings 12:7 "If you will be a servant to this people today and serve them, and speak good words to them when you answer them, then they will be your servants forever."

Rehoboam also consulted the young men he'd grown up with, who advised:

1 Kings 12:10-11 "Thus shall you speak to this people... 'My little finger is thicker than my father's thighs. And now, whereas my father laid on you a heavy yoke, I will add to your yoke.'"

Rehoboam chose the counsel that fed his ego. He wanted to show strength, assert dominance, prove he wasn't weak. The result? The kingdom split. Ten tribes walked away. His leadership collapsed because he chose the counsel that made him feel powerful instead of the counsel that was true. This is the danger. Not that you seek counsel, but that you only accept the counsel you wanted to hear in the first place.

The Application: Building a Culture Where People Actually Speak

You can SAY you want input all day long, but if your team doesn't believe you mean it, they'll stay quiet.

Here's how you build a culture where "best answer wins" actually functions:

1. Prove You Can Handle Being Wrong

The junior developer only spoke up because he'd watched me admit I was wrong before. If I had a pattern of defending my ideas even when they were flawed, he would have stayed silent.

You build this credibility in small moments:

- Someone points out a flaw in your logic in a meeting. Do you get defensive or say "good catch"?

- A direct report proposes a better approach than yours. Do you claim their idea or credit them?

- You make a decision that doesn't work out. Do you blame others or own it?

Every time you handle correction with humility, you're building permission for people to challenge you in the future.

2. Ask Questions, Not Leading Questions

There's a difference between:

- "What am I missing?" (genuine question)

- "Don't you think this is the right approach?" (leading question seeking validation)

The first invites challenge. The second invites agreement.
I've learned to ask:

- "What's the strongest argument AGAINST this approach?"

- "If you were designing this from scratch, would you do it differently?"

- "What would make this fail?"

These questions surface objections before they become production problems.

3. Explain Your Reasoning, Especially When You Overrule

Sometimes I hear the input and still make a different call. When that happens, I owe the team an explanation.

Not "I hear you, but we're going with my approach." That shuts down future input.

Instead: "I hear what you're saying about X. Here's why I'm prioritizing Y over X in this case: [specific reasoning]. If Y turns out to be less important than we think, we'll revisit."

This does two things:

- Shows you actually considered their input (you're not just dismissing it)

- Gives them the framework for understanding future decisions

4. Change Your Mind Publicly When New Information Emerges

This is the hardest one. You make a decision. You've explained your reasoning. The team is aligned. Then new data comes in that contradicts your assumptions. Do you double down to save face, or do you say "I was working with incomplete information, here's what changed"?

I've learned to say: "Last week I said we're doing X. Since then we learned Y. Given Y, I think Z is actually better. Here's why."

The team sees that you care more about getting it right than being right. That's when "best answer wins" becomes real.

The Rough Edge: When You Struggle to Hear Certain People

I need to be honest about something. I say "best answer wins regardless of source." I believe that's true. I struggle to actually live it when the source is someone I've written off.

The Favorites Problem

I have favorites. Everyone does. We talk about this more in Chapter 14. There are people on my team whose input I trust more. People who've demonstrated good judgment over time. People I naturally gravitate toward when I need counsel. That's not necessarily wrong.

Proverbs talks about this:

> Proverbs 13:20 "Walk with the wise and become wise,
> for a companion of fools suffers harm."

Jesus himself had an inner circle. Peter, James, and John got access to moments the other disciples didn't. (Matthew 17:1, Mark 5:37, Mark 14:33) So having trusted advisors isn't the problem. The problem is when I stop listening to people outside that circle because they're not in the circle.

The question I have to keep asking myself: Are my favorites based on character and competence, or just people who think like me? If it's the latter, I'm not getting diverse input. I'm getting an echo chamber with extra steps.

The Track Record Problem

Here's where it gets harder. There are people on my team with bad track records. They've made poor calls in the past. Their judgment has been consistently off. When they speak up in a meeting, my internal response is: "Yeah, but you were wrong about X, Y, and Z, so why should I listen now?" I don't say that out loud, but I feel it, and I know it affects how seriously I take their input.

Proverbs seems to validate this:

> **Proverbs 13:20** "Whoever walks with the wise becomes wise, but the companion of fools will suffer harm."

> **Proverbs 23:9** "Do not speak in the hearing of a fool, for he will despise the good sense of your words."

So there's biblical warrant for being selective about whose counsel you seek. Here's the tension: What if I've labeled them a fool because they disagreed with me, not because they actually lack wisdom? What if their track record is bad because I've been measuring it by my preferences, not by actual outcomes? What if the thing they're right about is the exact thing I need to hear, and I'm dismissing it because of who's saying it?

The Balaam's Donkey Problem

Here's a weird Old Testament story that keeps me honest. Balaam is a prophet. He's riding his donkey to go curse Israel. An angel blocks the road with a sword, but Balaam can't see it. The donkey can. The donkey keeps swerving off the road to avoid the angel. Balaam keeps beating the donkey, frustrated that it won't go straight.

Finally, God opens the donkey's mouth and it speaks:

> Numbers 22:28 "What have I done to you, that you have struck me these three times?"

Eventually God opens Balaam's eyes and he sees the angel. The donkey was right. Balaam was wrong and Balaam was about to die because he wouldn't listen to the donkey.

The point: God can use anyone to speak truth to you. Even sources you wouldn't expect. Even the person with the bad track record. Even the junior developer who's only been here six months. Even the one you've mentally written off. The message matters more than the messenger.

What I'm Learning

I'm not claiming I've mastered this. I haven't.

I'm learning to ask myself:

- Is their input wrong, or just different from what I expected?

- Am I dismissing it because of bad logic, or because of who said it?

- Can I separate the message from the messenger long enough to evaluate it on merit?

Sometimes the answer is: "No, their input is actually bad. Their track record is bad for a reason."

Sometimes the answer is: "I almost missed something important because I wasn't willing to hear it from them."

The goal isn't to treat all input equally. Some people have earned more trust. That's legitimate. The goal is to make sure I'm evaluating input on merit, not just on whether it comes from someone in my inner circle.

The Secular Translation: Why Diverse Input Produces Better Outcomes

If you're reading this as a non-Christian leader wondering if this is just "spiritual decision-making," let me be direct: this works because it's true, not because it's religious. Organizations with diverse perspectives make better decisions. That's not a biblical claim; it's a research-backed reality.

Homogeneous teams make faster decisions, but they also make more predictable mistakes, because everyone's blind spots align. Diverse teams, teams where the best answer actually wins regardless of source, usually catch errors before they become disasters.

The junior developer who spotted the flaw in my API design? He caught it because he was NEW. He didn't have the same assumptions I had. His lack of experience was actually an advantage, because he could see what I'd stopped noticing.

The question for you isn't "do I believe the Bible?" The question is: "Am I actually listening to input that challenges me, or just input that confirms what I already believe?"

Most leaders say they want diverse input. What they actually want is unanimous agreement. "Best answer wins" requires you to lose sometimes and that's uncomfortable. The alternative is worse: making avoidable mistakes because you only listened to people who think like you.

The Connection to the Framework

Remember the four-part framework:

    1. **Humility** - "Who am I to judge? What am I missing?"

2. **Whole Counsel** - "What's the complete human and business impact?"

3. **Restoration or Protection** - "Can this be fixed or does someone need defending?"

4. **Moral Intuition** - "Does this feel right based on principles, not politics?"

"Best answer wins" directly supports all four:

1. **Humility:** Seeking counsel assumes you might be wrong. It forces you to ask "what am I missing?"

2. **Whole Counsel:** Different people see different angles. The junior developer saw the edge case I missed. Diverse input gives you fuller counsel.

3. **Restoration:** When you're willing to change your mind based on new information, you're choosing truth over ego. That's restorative, not defensive.

4. **Moral Intuition:** Input from people you trust helps calibrate your moral intuition. Iron sharpens iron.

Here's the key: this only works if you're **actually willing to be wrong.** If you're seeking input just to check a box, people will stop giving it and you'll be stuck with your own blind spots.

The Practical Takeaway

If you take one thing from this chapter, take this:

Leadership isn't about having all the answers. It's about being secure enough to seek them from others.

Seek input before you decide. Best answer wins, regardless of source. When the room is split, make the call, but always explain why. Be willing to change your mind when new information emerges. The leader who can say "I was wrong, you were right" builds more trust than the leader who's never wrong. The team that knows the best answer wins will speak up. The team that knows only the boss's answer wins will stay quiet. You can't afford a quiet team. Not when production is down. Not when the architecture is flawed. Not when your plan has a fatal flaw that everyone can see except you.

Proverbs 15:22 "Without counsel plans fail, but with many advisers they succeed."

Seek counsel. Make the call. Change your mind when you're wrong. Lead accordingly.

Reflection Questions

1. Think about your last major decision. Did you seek input before deciding, or announce your decision and call it "collaboration"?

2. When was the last time someone challenged your idea and you changed your mind? How did that feel? What did it teach your team?

3. Who are your "favorites"? Are they people who've earned trust through demonstrated judgment, or just people who

agree with you?

4. Is there someone on your team whose input you consistently dismiss? Why? Is it their track record, or your ego?

Chapter Twelve

The Reputation You Build When No One's Watching

T hose women didn't spontaneously decide I was trustworthy the moment they walked into my office to report harassment. They'd been watching me for months.

They'd seen how I handled the junior analyst who deleted production data. They'd watched me correct the salesman in front of the client instead of letting the lies stand. They'd noticed a thousand tiny moments that added up to a reputation: *This person can be trusted with something this important.*

Crisis trust doesn't start in the crisis. It starts in the ordinary Tuesday afternoon when no one's paying attention and nothing's on fire. It starts in the decisions you make when there's no audience, no applause, no immediate consequence for choosing the easy path over the right one. The reputation you build when no one's watching becomes the foundation for what people trust you with when everyone's watching.

The Small Moments That Built Crisis Trust

I didn't consciously set out to build a reputation that would make people feel safe reporting harassment. I wasn't running some long-term PR campaign for my character. I was just trying to lead well, day by day, decision by decision. Leadership isn't about the big dramatic moments. Those are just the visible tests of what you've been building in private. Leadership is about a thousand small decisions that most people never see but everyone eventually feels.

Crediting Others for Their Ideas

I learned this one from watching ego destroy collaboration. When someone on your team comes up with a solution to a problem, and you present it in the next leadership meeting, you have a choice: Take credit yourself, or name the person who actually thought of it. The first option makes you look smart. The second option makes your team feel valued.

I made it a rule: If someone else had the idea, I said their name when I presented it. Every time. Even when it was inconvenient. Even when I'd refined the idea so much that it felt partially mine. Even when no one was asking.

"Sarah figured out we could batch the overnight jobs to reduce server load by 30%. Here's how she's proposing we implement it."

Not, "We figured out a way to reduce server load." Not, "I've been looking at our overnight jobs and found a solution."

Sarah's idea. Sarah's name. Sarah's credit.

It cost me nothing. It bought me everything. When people eventually came to me with serious concerns, with harassment reports, with problems that required trust, they already knew I wasn't going to take credit for handling it well or make it about me. They knew I saw people, not just problems. They knew I gave credit where it was due, which meant they could trust me to give weight to their stories even when uncomfortable. Trust built in small moments pays dividends in crises.

Admitting When You Don't Know

I spent the first few years of my career terrified that someone would discover I didn't know everything.

Then I realized: everyone already knows you don't know everything. Pretending you do just makes you look insecure.

So I started saying:

- "I don't know, but let me find out."

- "That's not my area of expertise, who should we ask?"

- "I'm not sure, what do you think?"

The first few times I admitted ignorance in front of my team, I felt exposed. Vulnerable. Like I'd just handed them ammunition to undermine my authority. The opposite happened. They started trusting my judgment more, not less. When I *did* say I knew something, they believed me. My credibility went up because my certainty wasn't constant. I wasn't the leader who had an opinion on everything, I was the leader who was honest about what I knew and what I didn't.

When those women came to me with their harassment concerns, they weren't worried I'd pretend to understand their experience or mansplain how they should feel. They knew I'd listen before I assumed. They knew I'd admit when I needed to learn more before making a decision. Intellectual humility creates emotional safety.

Listening More Than Talking

This is harder than it sounds. I like to talk. I'm good at it. I've got strong opinions. I can articulate solutions quickly. One of my working geniuses is Galvanizing people around an idea. For years, I thought that's what leadership was: having the answer and communicating it clearly.

Then I realized the people who worked for me stopped bringing me problems. They just started implementing whatever I'd said, even when they knew it wouldn't work. I'd trained them to wait for my pronouncement instead of thinking for themselves.

So I started a new discipline: In any conversation, I'd let the other person talk first and I'd wait until they were completely finished before I responded. No interrupting. No "Yeah, but..." in the middle of their sentence. No formulating my response while they were still talking.

Just listening. Actually listening. It felt slow. Inefficient. Like I was wasting time when I could have just told them the answer five minutes ago. Something shifted. People started bringing me better information. They'd think through problems more thoroughly before coming to me because they knew I'd ask follow-up questions. They'd propose solutions instead of just reporting issues.

When the harassment reports came, those women knew they'd get a full hearing. Not a quick dismissal. Not an interruption with excuses or explanations. They knew I'd listen to the whole story before I reacted. They'd seen me do it a thousand times in situations that mattered far less.

Explaining Your Reasoning

I learned this one from the absentee king, the boss who worked from home while requiring everyone else on-site. He'd make decisions and never explain why. Just mandates from on high. Do this. Don't do that. Because I said so. It bred resentment and cynicism. Every decision felt arbitrary. Like he was just flexing authority instead of actually leading.

So when I became a leader, I made a rule: If I'm making the call, especially when it's not the popular call, I explain *why*. Not to justify myself. Not to beg for approval. Just to treat people like adults who deserve to understand the reasoning behind decisions that affect them.

"I know you all want to work from home more, but here's why I need you on-site three days a week: our collaboration quality drops when we're remote, and the client has specifically requested more face time. I hear you, I understand the inconvenience, but here's the trade-off I'm making and why."

Sometimes they agreed with my reasoning. Sometimes they didn't, but they never felt like I was hiding something or pulling rank just because I could. When I had to make the hard call about the inappropriate employee, and people asked why it took three conversations before termination, I could explain: "I don't fire people for mistakes or rough edges. I fire them when they refuse to change after multiple opportunities. Here's the pattern I saw. Here's the progressive discipline we followed. Here's why protection became necessary."

Transparency builds trust. Secrecy builds suspicion.

Treating People With Dignity Regardless of Rank

The receptionist at the front desk. The custodian who emptied the trash cans. The intern who'd been there two weeks. The junior developer fresh out of bootcamp. I tried to treat every one of them with the same respect I gave the CEO.

Not in some performative "I'm a good person" way. Just in the basic human way: eye contact, real conversation, remembering their names, asking how they're doing and actually listening to the answer.

I learned this one from my grandfather. He was a lumberjack who ran a sawmill in a small Idaho town, the kind of place where everyone knew your name and your business, personal and professional. He could be stern when he needed to be, but he was one of the most gentle men I've ever known. Worked with his hands his whole life, never had a fancy title or made a lot of money, but he treated everyone with respect, from the bank president to the guy who pumped his gas and people loved him for it.

He taught me: how you treat people who can't do anything for you reveals who you actually are.

So I made it a point to learn names. To ask the receptionist how her daughter's recital went. To thank the custodian by name when he stayed late to help set up for an event. To treat the intern's questions like they mattered as much as the senior architect's. It cost me nothing but a few minutes of attention, but people noticed.

When harassment reports came from women who weren't in leadership positions, who didn't have power or status, they already knew

I wouldn't dismiss them because of their rank. They knew I'd treated them with dignity when it didn't benefit me. They could trust I'd treat their concerns with the same weight I'd give anyone else. You can't fake this in the moment. It has to be your default.

Keeping Confidence

This is the non-negotiable. If someone tells you something in confidence, you keep it. Period. No exceptions. No "I won't say where I heard this, but..." No strategic leaking to build alliances. No using privileged information to make yourself look smart.

You keep your mouth shut. I learned this the hard way from the trust-breaker boss who promised confidentiality, tore up my email to prove it, then betrayed me fifteen minutes later. I swore I'd never do that to someone else.

So I developed a reputation: If you told me something in confidence, it stayed with me. Even when it would have been politically advantageous to share it. Even when keeping quiet made me look uninformed or out of the loop.

The cost was occasionally looking less informed than I actually was. The benefit was people trusted me with information they wouldn't tell anyone else.

When those women came to report harassment, they already knew their confidence was safe. They'd watched me keep other people's secrets. They'd never heard me gossip or share things I shouldn't. They knew the story wouldn't leave my office unless they wanted it to.

That trust, built over months of keeping my word in small things, made it possible for them to trust me with something this big.

Being Present in the Trenches

I work from home. Most of my directives go through Microsoft Teams, but I'm not the kind of remote CTO who hides behind Teams messages and disappears when things get hard.

I'm on camera. Face-to-face via webcam. Available. Not because I don't trust my team, but because I believe leadership is presence, and presence isn't about physical location, it's about engagement. You can't lead people you're not with, even if "with" means on a video call. You can't understand problems you don't see. You can't build relationships from a distance, but distance doesn't have to mean disengagement.

So I showed up. Virtually, but consistently. When the database went down at 9 PM, I was on the call with the team troubleshooting. When we had a difficult client meeting, I was on camera with them. When someone needed help debugging a nasty production issue, I rolled up my sleeves and dove into the code with them, screen-sharing and pair programming remotely.

When I needed to be on-site, I was. Not every day, but when it mattered. When the team needed face-to-face time, when the client required it, when the situation called for physical presence, I didn't hide behind "I work from home." Not micromanaging. Just present. Available. In it with them, even if "with them" meant through a screen most days.

When crisis hit, when people needed a leader who understood the full weight of what they were facing, they didn't have to wonder if I'd get it. They knew I'd been in the trenches with them all along. Engagement builds trust. Disengagement breeds doubt.

The Biblical Foundation

Luke 16:10 is one of those verses that sounds simple until you realize how much weight it carries:

> **Luke 16:10** *"One who is faithful in a very little is also faithful in much, and one who is dishonest in a very little is also dishonest in much."*

Jesus is teaching about stewardship, about how you handle what's been entrusted to you and his principle is this: the small things reveal your character. How you handle the little stuff is how you'll handle the big stuff.

You don't suddenly become trustworthy when the stakes are high. You're trustworthy in the crisis because you were trustworthy in a thousand small moments leading up to it.

The women who reported harassment to me weren't taking a leap of faith. They'd watched me be faithful in little things, so they trusted me to be faithful in much.

> **Proverbs 22:1** *"A good name is to be chosen rather than great riches."*

Your reputation, your name, the thing people associate with you when they hear it, that's more valuable than money because money can't buy trust. You can't purchase a reputation for integrity. You can only build it, slowly, through consistent faithfulness over time.

1 Timothy 3:7 talks about leaders needing "a good reputation with outsiders." Not just with people who like you or report to you. With everyone because your character, or lack of it, is visible to everyone. The way you treat the custodian when you think no one important is

watching tells people more about you than the speech you give at the leadership summit.

This isn't about performance. It's about consistency. Character isn't what you do when the spotlight's on you. It's what you do when no one's watching, or more accurately, it's what you do when you think no one's watching, but someone always is.

The Connection to Everything Else

Remember the junior analyst who deleted production data? That moment worked because I'd already built a reputation for giving people grace when they made honest mistakes. My team had seen me admit my own failures. They'd watched me treat mistakes as learning opportunities instead of firing offenses.

So when Priya made that catastrophic error, and I chose restoration over punishment, it wasn't surprising to my team. It was consistent. They'd seen me be faithful in the little things: admitting when I was wrong, crediting others, listening more than talking. That faithfulness in small moments gave me credibility in the big one.

The harassment reports? Those happened because I'd built a reputation for protecting vulnerable people, for keeping confidence, for treating everyone with dignity regardless of rank. I didn't know I was building that reputation. I was just trying to lead well, but the small decisions added up.

The sales meeting where I corrected the lies? That worked because I'd already established a reputation for truth-telling. My team knew I wouldn't let dishonesty slide in private meetings, so when I did it in front of a client, it was consistent. The client could trust me because they could see I valued truth more than the deal.

Every one of those crisis moments was built on a foundation of small decisions that no one was tracking, no one was applauding, no one was even noticing in the moment. Cumulatively? They created a reputation and that reputation became the basis for trust when it mattered most.

The Secular Translation

If you're not tracking with the Biblical stuff, let me put it in business terms: reputation is a lagging indicator of consistency. You can't build a trustworthy reputation in a moment. It's the cumulative effect of aligned behavior over time. Every small decision either deposits into or withdraws from your credibility account.

Organizational psychologists call this "behavioral integrity": the alignment between what you say and what you do, between your stated values and your actual decisions. Study after study shows it's one of the strongest predictors of leadership effectiveness.

Why? Because people are constantly watching you, even when you don't think they are. They're not listening to your speeches about integrity, they're watching how you handle the intern's idea in the team meeting. They're not impressed by your stated values on the wall, they're paying attention to whether you keep your word when it's inconvenient.

The small moments reveal your actual operating system and once people see your operating system, they know what to expect from you when the pressure's on.

That's why those women trusted me with harassment reports. Not because I said the right things, but because they'd seen my operating system. They knew what I valued because they'd watched me make decisions that revealed it. Your reputation isn't what you say about yourself. It's what your consistent behavior teaches people to expect from you.

The Hard Truth

I didn't get this right all the time. I still don't. There were moments when I took credit for someone else's idea because it made me look good. Times when I pretended to know something I didn't because admitting ignorance felt weak. Conversations where I talked more than I listened because I was impatient or thought I knew better.

I've broken confidence. Not often, but it's happened, and when it does I immediately apologize and ask for forgiveness. I've treated people with less dignity than they deserved because I was stressed or frustrated or just not paying attention. The small decisions that build reputation? I've failed at every one of them at some point.

Here's the thing: consistency doesn't mean perfection. It means the pattern over time. It means when you fail, you own it, apologize, and try to do better next time. It means the trajectory of your character is toward faithfulness, even if you stumble along the way.

People aren't looking for perfect leaders. They're looking for consistent ones. Leaders who are predictable in their values even if they're not flawless in their execution.

I've had to apologize to team members for snapping at them when I was frustrated. I've had to circle back and credit someone I forgot to mention in a meeting. I've had to admit I broke confidence when I shouldn't have and rebuild trust the hard way. I have been humbled when I have to ask for forgiveness.

Those failures didn't destroy my reputation because the pattern was still clear: when I messed up, I owned it. That's a form of consistency too.

The Long View

The reputation you build when no one's watching doesn't pay dividends immediately. It's a long-term investment. You credit someone else's idea in a Tuesday meeting, and nothing changes. You admit you don't know something, and the meeting moves on. You treat the custodian with respect, and no one applauds. Six months later, when you need your team to trust you with a difficult decision, they do. You've made a thousand small deposits into the credibility account and when you need to make a withdrawal, there's something there to draw from.

> **Galatians 6:9** *"Let us not grow weary of doing good, for in due season we will reap, if we do not give up."*

The "due season" isn't immediate. It's not transactional. You don't get instant returns on character investments. Over time, faithfulness in small things compounds into trust in big things. Those women didn't walk into my office on a random Tuesday and suddenly decide I was trustworthy enough to report harassment to. They'd been making that assessment for months, watching how I led when nothing was on fire.

When they needed someone they could trust with something that serious, they didn't have to take a leap of faith. The foundation was already there. That's the power of the long view: you build reputation slowly, through a thousand small decisions no one's tracking, so when the crisis comes and everyone's watching, you've already earned the trust you need. You can't buy it. You can't fake it. You can only build it.

One small decision at a time. One moment of faithfulness when no one's looking. One opportunity to be consistent when it would be easier not to be. Eventually, if you don't give up, the small things add up to something that holds when the pressure's on. The question isn't whether people are watching you. They are. Always. The question is: what are they learning about you when you think no one's paying attention? That's the reputation you'll have when you need it most.

Part 4

I could have ended the book with Part 3. Given you a framework, shown you it works, demonstrated how to build culture through daily decisions. Left you with the impression I've got this figured out. That would be a lie.

The truth is, I'm still being shaped, we all are. I still have rough edges that scrape against the leader I want to be. I still become someone I'm not proud of when I'm frustrated and tired and done with people's excuses. I still struggle to receive feedback from people whose judgment I don't respect. I still have favorites, and I'm not always sure if it's wisdom or partiality.

This section is the honest part most leadership books skip. The gap between principle and practice. The tension between who you are and who you're becoming. The moments when you know what's right but you choose what's comfortable. The slow, grinding work of character formation that doesn't happen in crisis but in the daily discipline of trying again after you've failed.

If you're looking for a leadership book that presents a polished image of someone who's arrived, this section will disappoint you. If you're looking for honesty about what it actually looks like to pursue principled leadership while still being shaped by it, while still wrestling with your own limitations, while still growing into someone better than you are today, then this is for you.

The goal isn't perfection. It's faithfulness, and faithfulness means being honest about where you're still a work in progress.

Chapter Thirteen

When Frustration Wins

I need to tell you something that might undermine everything I've written so far. I gave grace to the junior analyst who deleted production data. I protected the women who reported harassment. I corrected the salesman's lies in front of the client. I've built a framework for leadership that prioritizes humility, context, restoration, and moral intuition, but I still get frustrated when people drop the ball.

Not the "this is a teaching moment" kind of frustration. The "I'm fighting the urge to be unloving" kind. The kind where my face gives me away before my words do. The kind where I get quiet, and everyone in the room knows I'm not happy, even if I'm trying to be gracious about it. The kind where my wife can tell from across the house that a work call didn't go well because of how hard I'm typing.

I can have all the right theological frameworks in the world, quote all the right verses about patience and gentleness, and still feel the heat rising when someone misses a deadline they promised to hit, or delivers work that's half of what was agreed on, or drops a commitment that I was counting on.

This chapter is about the gap between the leader I want to be and the leader I am on a Tuesday afternoon when the third person in a row has failed to deliver what they said they would.

The Reality Check

Here's what I've noticed about myself: I handle catastrophic failures better than I handle chronic mediocrity.

The junior analyst deleting production data? That was a one-time mistake, clear consequences, immediate remorse, fixable with restoration. I could extend grace because it was an honest error from someone who genuinely cared and messed up.

The person who consistently delivers 70% of what they committed to? The one who always has an excuse, always has a reason why this time was different, always promises to do better next time but never actually does? That person tests every ounce of patience I have.

The team member who shows up late to meetings, unprepared, and then acts like it's no big deal? The one who treats deadlines as suggestions and commitments as aspirations? I struggle to extend the same grace.

I know why: high performers struggle with other people's incompetence, or what looks like incompetence, or what might just be a different standard of excellence that doesn't match mine.

I hold myself to a certain standard. I work hard. I meet my commitments. I don't make promises I can't keep and when other people don't operate the same way, especially people I'm depending on, the frustration builds. I get quiet. My face hardens. I start responding in shorter sentences and anyone who knows me can tell I'm annoyed, even if I'm trying not to be. My wife knows the look. My direct reports have learned to recognize it. It's not yelling, it's not blowing up, but it's not exactly grace under pressure either.

The Struggle With My Own Reactions

The frustration itself isn't the problem. The problem is what I'm tempted to do with it. I'm tempted to be short with people. Dismissive. To stop giving them the benefit of the doubt. To mentally write them off as "not serious" or "not capable" and stop investing in their growth.

I'm tempted to say things I know will cut, even if they're technically true. To deliver feedback with an edge that's more about venting my frustration than helping them improve. I'm tempted to stop explaining my reasoning and just start issuing directives. To shift from collaborative leadership to "just do what I said" leadership because I'm tired of people not getting it.

The junior analyst? I extended grace because I saw her remorse, her care, her genuine devastation at having failed. The framework kicked in naturally: humility, whole counsel, restoration, but the person who chronically underdelivers and doesn't seem to care? I have to fight to apply the same framework because my gut reaction isn't "How can I restore this person?" It's "How do I get this person to stop wasting my time?" I know that's not right. I know that's not who I want to be, but it's where my mind goes when frustration builds.

The Biblical Tension

Here's where it gets complicated: the Bible doesn't say all anger is sin.

Ephesians 4:26 says, *"Be angry and do not sin; do not let the sun go down on your anger."*

Be angry and do not sin. Paul's not saying don't be angry. He's saying there's a way to be angry that doesn't cross into sin. Which means there's such a thing as righteous anger, justified frustration at real problems that need to be addressed.

Jesus got angry. When he saw the money changers turning the temple into a marketplace, exploiting the poor and making worship transactional, he didn't calmly ask them to reconsider their business model. He flipped tables. He drove them out with a whip (John 2:13-17).

That was righteous anger. Anger at injustice. Anger at something that violated what was sacred. Here's the question I have to ask myself when I'm frustrated: Is this righteous anger, or is this just my ego being bruised because someone didn't meet my expectations? Am I angry because something genuinely wrong happened, or am I angry because my plan got disrupted? Am I frustrated at the person, or am I frustrated at the situation? Is this conviction, or is this just preference?

The Questions I Have to Ask

When I feel that frustration rising, when my face is getting hard and my responses are getting short, I've learned to force myself to stop and ask a few questions before I react.

Question 1: Is the frustration about their failure or my plan?

This is the hardest one to answer honestly.

When someone misses a deadline, am I frustrated because they broke a commitment (which is a real problem), or am I frustrated because *I* was counting on that deadline and now *my* plans are disrupted? If it's the latter, that's not righteous anger. That's just me being annoyed that the universe didn't cooperate with my schedule.

There's a difference between someone failing to do what they committed to do (legitimate concern) and someone not doing what I wanted in the way I wanted it done (control issue). The first one deserves a conversation. The second one deserves some self-reflection on why I think my preferences are the standard everyone should meet.

Question 2: Are they actually failing, or are they just not meeting my standard?

I have high standards. I know this about myself. I'm demanding. I expect a lot from people because I expect a lot from myself.

But here's the question I have to ask: Am I holding myself accountable to God's standard before I hold others accountable to mine? If I'm frustrated that someone isn't meeting my expectations while I'm simultaneously falling short of God's expectations for how I treat people, that's hypocrisy. That's the Pharisee measuring everyone else's grain while his own scales are rigged.

> **Matthew 7:3-5** *"Why do you see the speck that is in your brother's eye, but do not notice the log that is in your own eye? Or how can you say to your brother, 'Let me take the speck out of your eye,' when there is the log in your own eye? You hypocrite, first take the log out of your*

own eye, and then you will see clearly to take the speck
out of your brother's eye."

When I'm frustrated with someone's performance, am I meeting God's standard for patience? For kindness? For gentleness in correction, or am I expecting them to meet my standard while I ignore His? This is where humility has to kick in: Am I frustrated because they're genuinely underperforming, or am I frustrated because they're not performing the way *I* would perform?

My standard isn't the only valid standard and just because someone doesn't operate at my pace or my level of intensity doesn't mean they're failing. It might just mean they're not me. If I'm holding everyone to "Justin's (insert your name here) standard" instead of "the actual agreed-upon standard," that's on me, not them. If I'm holding them to any standard while ignoring God's standard for how I lead them, that's worse than a management problem. That's a character problem.

Question 3: Have I given them what they need to succeed?

This is the accountability question I have to ask myself. When someone consistently underdelivers, is it because they're incapable, or is it because I haven't given them the resources, clarity, or support they need?

Did I explain the expectations clearly? Did I give them the training they needed? Did I check in along the way, or did I just assume they'd figure it out? Sometimes the person I'm frustrated with isn't the problem. I'm the problem. I set them up to fail by not leading well, and now I'm frustrated that they failed. That's not righteous anger. That's me being mad about my own leadership failure and projecting it onto them.

Question 4: Is this a pattern or a moment?

The junior analyst was a moment. One catastrophic mistake from an otherwise excellent employee. That's easy to extend grace to. What about the person who's consistently late, consistently unprepared, consistently delivering less than what was agreed on? That's a pattern and patterns need to be addressed, not excused. The question is: Am I addressing the pattern with the goal of restoration, or am I just venting my frustration? If it's the latter, I'm not leading. I'm just punishing.

The Growth I'm Still Pursuing

I don't have this figured out. I wish I could tell you I've mastered the tension between grace and accountability, that I've learned to feel frustration without letting it turn into sin. I haven't. I'm learning to recognize the warning signs. The tightness in my chest. The shortness in my responses. The face that my wife and my team have learned to read. When I catch myself, I've learned to do a few things:

1. Step away before I respond

If I'm frustrated, I don't respond immediately. I don't send that email. I don't make that call. I give myself time to process whether the frustration is data (there's a real problem here that needs addressing) or emotion (I'm annoyed and need to deal with my own reaction first).

The email I write when I'm frustrated always needs to be rewritten. Always. So I've learned to write it, save it as a draft, and come back to it later when I've cooled down or not write it at all.

2. Separate the person from the problem

This is straight from the framework: whole counsel. See the whole person, not just the failure. When someone drops the ball, I force myself to ask: What's going on in their life right now? Are they overwhelmed? Under-resourced? Dealing with something outside of work that's affecting their performance?

That doesn't excuse the failure, but it does change how I respond to it. The junior analyst was shaking on the call, devastated by her mistake. That context mattered. It turned my response from judgment to restoration. The person who chronically underdelivers, are they struggling with something I don't know about? Are they in over their head and too afraid to admit it? Are they dealing with a personal crisis that's draining their capacity? I can't extend grace if I don't see the full picture.

3. Ask whether this is conviction or preference

This is the moral intuition piece from the framework, but applied to my own reactions. When I'm frustrated, I have to ask: Is this frustration rooted in a principle that matters (integrity, honesty, commitment), or is it rooted in my preference for how things should be done? If it's conviction, I need to address it. If it's preference, I need to let it go.

The salesman lying to the client? That was conviction. Dishonesty violates something fundamental. I had to speak up. Someone organizing a project differently than I would? That's preference. I need to step back and let them lead their way, even if it's not how I'd do it.

4. Give myself grace while pursuing growth

When I'm frustrated with my own limitations I turn to Phillippians:

> **Philippians 3:12** *"Not that I have already obtained this or am already perfect, but I press on to make it my own, because Christ Jesus has made me his own."*

Paul, the apostle who wrote half the New Testament, the guy who planted churches across the Roman Empire, openly admits: I'm not perfect. I haven't arrived. I'm still pressing on. If Paul can admit he's still growing, I can too.

> **Philippians 1:6** *"And I am sure of this, that he who began a good work in you will bring it to completion at the day of Christ Jesus."*

God's still working on me. I'm not the finished product, and that means I'm going to have moments where frustration wins, where I don't respond the way I should, where the gap between who I want to be and who I am shows up in living color. That doesn't mean I get to excuse it, but it does mean I don't have to be paralyzed by it. I can own it, apologize when necessary, and keep pressing forward.

The Hard Conversations I've Had to Have

There have been times when I've had to circle back to someone and apologize for how I responded.

"Hey, I was short with you in that meeting. I was frustrated about the deadline, but that's not an excuse for how I spoke to you. I'm sorry."

Those conversations are humbling because they require me to admit I didn't live up to my own standard, let alone God's. They're also necessary, because if I'm going to lead with integrity, I can't just expect other people to own their failures while I hide mine.

> **James 5:16** *"Therefore, confess your sins to one another and pray for one another, that you may be healed."*

Confession isn't just vertical (me to God). It's horizontal (me to the people I've wronged), and sometimes the person I've wronged is the team member I snapped at because I was frustrated. Owning that doesn't undermine my leadership. It reinforces it. It shows my team that the standard I'm asking them to live by is the same standard I'm holding myself to.

When Frustration Is Actually Data

Here's the other side of this: sometimes frustration is telling you something important. Not all frustration is sinful. Sometimes it's your internal warning system alerting you to a real problem that needs to be addressed. When I'm consistently frustrated with the same person about the same issue, that's data. It means there's either a performance problem, a mismatch between their role and their capacity, or a misalignment between expectations and reality. Ignoring that data in the name of "grace" isn't actually grace. It's avoidance.

Grace doesn't mean pretending problems don't exist. It means addressing them with the goal of restoration instead of punishment. The inappropriate employee from Chapter 7? I was frustrated with him. Multiple times. I didn't just sit in my frustration and let it fester. I addressed it. Three times. Progressively. With clear expectations and consequences.

When restoration didn't work, protection became necessary, and that wasn't a failure of grace, it was grace applied in a different form: protecting the women on the team who deserved a safe workplace. Frustration can be a signal that something needs to change. The question is whether I'm responding to that signal by addressing the real issue, or just venting my annoyance.

The Ongoing Tension

I still struggle with this. Regularly. Just last week, I had a project derail because someone didn't deliver what they said they'd deliver. I felt that familiar tightness in my chest, the frustration building, the temptation to fire off a sharp email or cut them out of future projects.

I didn't. I stepped away. I processed. I asked the questions. Then I had a conversation that focused on what went wrong and how to fix it going forward, instead of just unloading my frustration on them. It was a fight. It required conscious effort to apply the framework instead of just reacting from emotion. That's the reality of leadership: the principles hold, but applying them when you're frustrated, tired, or just done with people's excuses is hard.

James 1:19-20 *"Know this, my beloved brothers: let every person be quick to hear, slow to speak, slow to anger; for the anger of man does not produce the righteousness of God."*

Quick to hear. Slow to speak. Slow to anger. I fail at this regularly. I'm often quick to speak, slow to hear, and faster to anger than I want to admit. The standard is still the standard. The fact that I struggle to meet it doesn't mean I stop trying. It just means I'm still being shaped.

What I'm Learning

The tension between grace and accountability isn't something you resolve. It's something you manage. High performers will always struggle with other people's failure to perform. That's not going away. The intensity that makes you good at what you do is the same intensity that makes you impatient when others don't share it.

I'm learning to distinguish between:

- Legitimate accountability (addressing real performance issues with the goal of restoration)

- Control issues (being frustrated that people don't operate the way I operate)

- Projection (being mad about my own failures and taking it out on others)

I'm learning to ask: Is this frustration about their failure, or my plan? Their incompetence, or my impatience? A real problem, or just a preference? I'm learning to give myself grace while still pursuing growth. To admit when I fail, apologize when I'm wrong, and keep pressing forward even when the gap between who I am and who I want to be feels discouragingly wide. The alternative is pretending I've arrived and that's a lie that helps no one.

The Secular Translation

If the Biblical framing doesn't resonate with you, let me put it in leadership terms: emotional intelligence includes the ability to recognize your own emotional triggers and manage your responses to them.

Self-aware leaders know when they're reacting from frustration versus responding from principle. They recognize the warning signs of their own stress responses and build in safeguards to prevent themselves from making decisions or sending communications they'll regret later.

The research on emotional regulation shows that leaders who can identify and manage their emotions are more effective than leaders who either suppress them entirely or let them drive their behavior unchecked. Frustration is data. It tells you something might be wrong. It's not automatically correct data. Sometimes it's telling you there's a real performance issue. Sometimes it's telling you that *you're* stressed and everything's annoying you more than it should. The skill is learning to discern which is which before you act on it.

The Long View

I don't know if I'll ever fully master this tension. I suspect I'll be wrestling with it for the rest of my leadership career. I'm not the same leader I was five years ago. I'm quicker to recognize when frustration is driving my responses. I'm better at stepping back before I react. I'm more willing to apologize when I get it wrong. That's growth. Not perfection, but progress.

If God's not done with me yet, if Philippians 1:6 is true and He's still working on me, then maybe the point isn't to have it all figured out. Maybe the point is to keep pressing forward. To keep applying the framework even when it's hard. To keep choosing grace over judgment, restoration over punishment, humility over ego.

Even on the days when frustration wins a round or two. Leadership isn't about being perfect. It's about being consistent in your values even when you're inconsistent in your execution. On the days when you fail, you own it, you learn from it, and you try again tomorrow.

If you take nothing else from this chapter, take this: The gap between the leader you want to be and the leader you are in the moment of frustration is where character is actually built. Not in the moments when grace comes easy, but in the moments when it doesn't. That's where you find out whether your principles are real or just words you say when it's convenient.

When you fail, when frustration wins and you respond poorly, that's not the end. Own it. Apologize. Learn from it and keep going. The goal isn't perfection. It's faithfulness over time, even when time includes a lot of messy, imperfect moments.

Chapter Fourteen

The People You've Written Off

I have a problem with receiving feedback from people I don't respect. If someone I trust, someone with a proven track record of good judgment, tells me I'm wrong about something, I can receive it. Not easily, because my ego still gets in the way, but I can at least consider it. I'll wrestle with it, pray about it, maybe even change my mind.

If someone I've mentally categorized as "consistently makes bad decisions" gives me feedback? My default reaction is dismissal. Not out loud, usually. I'm polite. I'll nod, say "I'll think about that," and then promptly ignore it. In my head, I've already run the calculation: This person's track record of judgment is poor, therefore their current input is probably also poor.

It follows logically and it's not entirely wrong. Track records do matter. Patterns of judgment do tell you something about someone's discernment. It's also dangerously close to arrogance. What I'm really saying is: "I've judged you and found you lacking, therefore I don't need to seriously consider what you're telling me." That's a problem. Sometimes the people I've written off are actually right.

The Tension

Here's where it gets complicated: Scripture seems to support both sides of this tension.

> **Proverbs 12:1** *"Whoever loves discipline loves knowledge, but he who hates reproof is stupid."*

Strong words. If you refuse to be corrected, you're a fool. No nuance, no qualifiers. Love discipline or be stupid. Those are the options.

> **Proverbs 23:9** *"Do not speak in the hearing of a fool, for he will despise the wisdom of your words."*

Wait, so which is it? Am I supposed to receive correction from everyone, or am I supposed to recognize that some people are fools whose input I should ignore? The answer, I think, is both. The tricky part is discerning which category the person in front of me actually falls into. Are they a fool whose opinion genuinely doesn't matter because they'll despise wisdom no matter how you present it? Or have I written them off as a fool because it's easier than admitting they might have a point?

The People I've Dismissed

I can think of specific people over the years who I mentally put in the "their opinion doesn't matter" category. The person who consistently made poor decisions about project priorities, who seemed to lack any sense of what mattered most. When they'd give me feedback about how I was handling something, I'd file it under "consider the source" and move on.

The employee who always seemed to be operating from emotion rather than logic, whose responses to situations felt reactive rather than thoughtful. When they'd challenge a decision I made, I'd internally roll my eyes and think, "Of course you don't agree, you never see the bigger picture."

The leader in another department who I'd watched mismanage their own team multiple times. When they'd offer input on how I should handle something in my department, my gut reaction was, "You can't even manage your own people, why would I listen to you about mine?"

Here's the uncomfortable truth: sometimes I was right. Sometimes their input *was* poor. Sometimes their track record of bad judgment did accurately predict that their current feedback was also misguided, but not always. The times when I dismissed good feedback because of who it came from, those are the times that haunt me.

When the Wrong Person Says the Right Thing

There was an employee, let's call him Jim, who drove me crazy. He was smart, but he had a tendency to overthink things to the point of paralysis. Where I'd see a decision that needed to be made quickly, he'd see seventeen different variables that needed to be analyzed first.

Where I'd see an acceptable level of risk, he'd see catastrophe waiting to happen.

We'd been through multiple projects together, and every time, his caution had slowed us down. We'd miss windows of opportunity because he wanted one more analysis, one more meeting, one more round of discussion. I'd grown impatient with him. Frustrated. If I'm honest, I'd mentally put him in the "overthinks everything and has poor judgment about what actually matters" category.

So when he raised concerns about a system architecture decision I was making, I didn't really listen. I heard him, but I didn't *listen*. I thought I knew what he was doing: overthinking again, seeing problems that weren't really problems, letting perfect be the enemy of good. I thanked him for his input and moved forward with my plan.

Three months later, we hit the exact problem he'd warned me about. The architecture decision I'd made created a bottleneck that was now costing us significant performance issues. It was fixable, but it required rework that could have been avoided if I'd listened to him in the first place.

He'd been right and I'd dismissed him because I'd categorized him as "the guy who overthinks everything." The issue wasn't that he overthought everything. The issue was that I'd decided his *pattern* of overthinking meant I could dismiss his *specific* input without seriously evaluating it. I'd written him off and it cost us.

The Question I Have to Ask

When someone I don't respect gives me feedback I don't want to hear, I've learned I need to ask myself a hard question:

Am I dismissing this input because it's genuinely bad, or because I don't like the messenger?

Can I separate the message from the messenger? This is harder than it sounds. We're wired to evaluate information based on the source. If someone we trust says something, we give it weight. If someone we don't trust says the same thing, we're skeptical. That's not entirely irrational. Credibility matters. Track records matter. If someone has consistently demonstrated poor judgment, it's reasonable to weigh their input accordingly.

It becomes a problem when I stop evaluating the actual content of what they're saying and just run it through my "is this person credible?" filter and move on. Even people with poor overall judgment can be right about specific things. Even people I don't respect can see things I'm missing. Even the person with the worst track record in the room might have the one piece of information or perspective that I actually need.

The Biblical Reality: God Uses Unlikely Sources

If I needed a reminder that God doesn't limit truth to people I respect, the story of Caiaphas should do it. John 11:49-52 tells this remarkable moment: Caiaphas was the high priest who wanted Jesus dead. He was actively plotting to have Jesus arrested and executed. He was, by any measure, hostile to everything Jesus represented.

Yet, in the middle of his scheming, he spoke prophecy.

> *John 11:49-50 "You know nothing at all. Nor do you understand that it is better for you that one man should die for the people, not that the whole nation should perish."*

He meant it as cold political calculation: better to kill one trou-
blemaker than risk Roman intervention, but John adds this stunning
commentary: *"He did not say this of his own accord, but being high priest
that year he prophesied that Jesus would die for the nation."*

Caiaphas spoke truth without even knowing it. God used the
mouth of Jesus's enemy to declare the theological reality of the gospel:
Jesus would die for the people, you, me, everyone. The person actively
working to destroy Jesus became the mouthpiece for the very truth he
was trying to silence.

If God can speak truth through someone hostile to His purpos-
es, He can certainly speak truth through the person I've written off
as having poor judgment. The question isn't whether the source is
credible. The question is whether the message is true. I can't answer
that question if I refuse to seriously consider the message because I've
already dismissed the messenger.

The Difference Between a Fool and a Different Perspective

Here's where I've had to grow: learning to distinguish between someone who is actually a fool (in the Biblical sense) and someone who just
has a different perspective or operates differently than I do.

> **Proverbs 26:4-5** *"Answer not a fool according to his
> folly, lest you be like him yourself. Answer a fool accord-
> ing to his folly, lest he be wise in his own eyes."*

Wait, so do I answer or not? Both verses are right next to each
other, seemingly contradicting. The point, I think, is discernment.

Sometimes engaging with a fool just drags you down to their level. Sometimes you need to answer them so they don't think their foolishness is actually wisdom.

The key question is: Are they actually a fool, or do I just think they're a fool because they disagree with me? Biblical foolishness isn't about intelligence. It's about a rejection of wisdom, a refusal to be taught, a commitment to one's own way regardless of truth.

> **Proverbs 18:2** *"A fool takes no pleasure in understanding, but only in expressing his opinion."*

That's different from someone who has a different opinion than mine. That's different from someone whose judgment I think is flawed. That's even different from someone who's made bad decisions in the past. A fool refuses to be corrected. They're not interested in truth, only in being right.

Someone who's willing to listen, who's open to being wrong, who's genuinely trying to think through a problem even if they're coming at it from a different angle than I am? That's not a fool. That's just someone I disagree with. Dismissing them because I've decided their judgment is inferior to mine? That's not discernment. That's arrogance.

What I'm Learning to Do

I haven't mastered this. I still have gut reactions of dismissal when certain people give me feedback, but I'm learning to build in a few safeguards to catch myself before I write someone off entirely.

1. Ask someone else I trust

When I receive feedback from someone I don't respect, I've started running it by someone I do respect. Not to validate my dismissal. To actually pressure-test the feedback.

"Hey, Jim raised this concern about the architecture decision. I'm tempted to dismiss it because I think he overthinks everything, but I want to make sure I'm not missing something. What do you think?"

That forces me to articulate the feedback clearly enough for someone else to evaluate. It gives me a second opinion from someone whose judgment I trust. Sometimes they confirm my instinct: "Yeah, that's overthinking. Move forward." Sometimes they say, "Actually, I think he's onto something." Either way, I'm not just relying on my own biased filter.

2. Evaluate the content, not just the source

I've started forcing myself to write down the actual content of the feedback, stripped of who said it. If Jim says, "This architecture will create a bottleneck under high load," I write that down. Then I evaluate it: Is that statement true or false? Not "Does Jim usually overthink?" but "Will this architecture create a bottleneck?" That forces me to engage with the message instead of just dismissing the messenger.

3. Consider whether they might see something I don't

This is the humility piece. When someone challenges a decision I've made, instead of immediately defending it or dismissing them, I try to ask: What might they be seeing that I'm missing? Even if their overall judgment is flawed, even if their track record is poor, is there a specific angle or concern they're raising that I haven't considered? I don't have to agree with their conclusion to take seriously the question they're raising.

4. Remember times I've been wrong

This is the most humbling exercise: thinking back to times when I was absolutely certain I was right, and I was wrong. Times when I dismissed feedback that turned out to be accurate. Times when my confidence in my own judgment blinded me to reality. Times when someone I didn't respect saw something I missed. If I've been wrong before, I can be wrong now. The person I'm tempted to dismiss might be the one bringing the perspective I actually need.

The Growth I'm Pursuing

> **Proverbs 15:31-32** "*The ear that listens to life-giving reproof will dwell among the wise. Whoever ignores instruction despises himself, but he who listens to reproof gains intelligence.*"

That's a sobering statement. When I ignore instruction, I'm not just dismissing the other person. I'm despising myself. I'm sabotaging my own growth because I've decided I don't need to hear from certain people. The verse doesn't say, "Listen to reproof from people you respect." It says whoever listens to reproof gains intelligence. The focus is on the listening, not on vetting the source first.

That doesn't mean I have to agree with everyone. It doesn't mean every piece of feedback is valid. It doesn't mean I can't discern that some people's judgment is better than others. It does mean I can't dismiss input without actually considering it just because I've decided the source isn't credible.

I'm learning, slowly, to separate message from messenger. To evaluate feedback on its merit, not just on who's delivering it. To be humble enough to admit that even people I don't respect might see things I don't. It's not natural for me. My default is still to categorize people: trustworthy input, untrustworthy input, worth listening to, not worth listening to. I'm trying to build in a pause. A moment to ask: Is this actually bad feedback, or do I just not like who it's coming from?

The times I've gotten this wrong, the times I've dismissed good input because I'd written off the person giving it, those are the mistakes that could have been avoided if I'd been willing to listen to someone I didn't want to hear from.

The Secular Translation

If you're not tracking with the Biblical framework, here's the business case: cognitive diversity improves decision-making. When everyone in the room thinks like you, you miss blind spots. When you only listen to people who share your perspective, you create an echo chamber. The best decisions come from evaluating multiple viewpoints, even viewpoints you disagree with.

Research on groupthink shows that teams make worse decisions when dissenting voices are silenced or dismissed. The person with the unpopular opinion, the one everyone else thinks is wrong, sometimes they're the only one seeing the problem clearly. If you've mentally categorized someone as "poor judgment, ignore their input," you've created a filter that might protect you from bad advice, but might also block you from seeing something you need to see. The skill isn't accepting all feedback equally. It's being able to evaluate feedback on its content rather than filtering it entirely based on the source.

The Hard Truth

I still struggle to receive feedback from people whose judgment I don't trust. That gut reaction of dismissal is still there. Just recently, someone I'd mentally written off raised a concern about a project approach I was taking. My immediate internal reaction was, "Here we go again, they don't understand what we're trying to do." I forced myself to pause. To write down what they were actually saying. To ask someone else I trusted what they thought.

They were partially right. Not entirely, their proposed solution wasn't great, but the concern they raised was valid. If I'd just dismissed them based on their track record, I'd have missed it. I'm not where I want to be on this. I'd love to tell you I've learned to receive all feedback with equal openness, that I evaluate every message purely on its merit with no bias about the messenger. That's not true. The bias is still there. The dismissiveness is still there.

I'm learning to catch it. To build in safeguards. To at least ask the question: Am I dismissing this because it's wrong, or because I don't like who said it? Sometimes, grudgingly, I'm learning that the person I least wanted to hear from is the one I most needed to listen to.

The Ongoing Tension

Proverbs 27:6 *"Faithful are the wounds of a friend;*
profuse are the kisses of an enemy."

The people who love you enough to tell you hard truths, even
when it's uncomfortable, those are your friends. The people who tell
you what you want to hear because they want to stay in your good
graces, those are not helping you. Here's the tension: sometimes the
hard truth comes from a friend you trust. Sometimes it comes from
someone you've written off.

If I only receive correction from people I like, I'm not actually open
to correction. I'm just open to affirmation from trusted sources. Real
humility means being willing to hear truth from anyone. Even people
I don't respect. Even people whose overall judgment I question. Even
people I've categorized as "doesn't get it."

God spoke truth through a donkey. He can certainly speak truth
through the person I've dismissed. If I refuse to even consider that
possibility, I'm not demonstrating discernment. I'm demonstrating
pride. If you take nothing else from this chapter, take this: The people
you've written off might be the ones you most need to hear from. Not
because they're always right. They're not, but because your willingness
to dismiss them reveals more about your humility, or lack thereof, than
it does about the quality of their input.

You don't have to agree with everyone. You don't have to give equal
weight to all feedback. Track records matter. Patterns of judgment
matter. If you've reached the point where you automatically dismiss
someone's input without actually evaluating it, you've crossed from
discernment into arrogance, and that's a blind spot that will cost you.

Chapter Fifteen

The Favorites Problem

I have favorites. I know I'm not supposed to admit that. Leaders are supposed to treat everyone equally, value all contributions the same, give everyone the same access and opportunity. We're supposed to be impartial, objective, fair. I have people I like more than others. People I trust more. People I go to first when I need input on something important. People who get more of my time, more of my attention, more opportunities to lead significant projects.

I try to be fair. I really do, but if I'm honest, it's probably obvious to everyone on my team who's in the inner circle and who's not. That bothers me because I know favoritism is destructive. I've seen it kill team morale. I've watched leaders play favorites and destroy trust across entire organizations. I've been on the outside of someone else's inner circle, and it's demoralizing. I also know that not all "favorites" are the same. There's a difference between unfair favoritism and earned trust. The question is: which one am I actually practicing?

The Distinction I Have to Make

Here's the tension: Jesus had favorites. That sounds wrong to say, almost heretical, but it's true. Jesus had an inner circle.

Out of all His followers, He chose twelve disciples. Out of those twelve, He was closer to some than others. Peter, James, and John went places and saw things the other disciples didn't. They were with Him on the Mount of Transfiguration (Matthew 17:1-8). They were with Him in the Garden of Gethsemane when He prayed before His crucifixion (Matthew 26:36-46).

The other disciples weren't invited. Just the inner three. Even within that inner three, John refers to himself as "the disciple whom Jesus loved" (John 13:23). Not that Jesus didn't love the others, but there was clearly a special closeness there. Was that favoritism? Or was that something else?

Paul had an inner circle too. Timothy, Silas, Titus, Barnabas (before they split), Luke. These were the people he traveled with, trusted with significant ministry, wrote letters to, invested in personally. He had hundreds, maybe thousands, of people in the churches he planted, but these few got his focused attention and mentorship.

David had his mighty men (2 Samuel 23:8-39). A specific group of warriors who'd proven themselves in battle, earned his trust, and got access to him that others didn't.

So if Jesus, Paul, and David all had inner circles, all had people they were closer to and trusted more, maybe the issue isn't having favorites. Maybe the issue is what those favorites are based on. James condemns favoritism, but the kind of favoritism James is talking about is specific:

> *James 2:1-9* "*My brothers, show no partiality as you hold the faith in our Lord Jesus Christ, the Lord of glory.*

For if a man wearing a gold ring and fine clothing comes into your assembly, and a poor man in shabby clothing also comes in, and if you pay attention to the one who wears the fine clothing... have you not then made distinctions among yourselves and become judges with evil thoughts?"

James is condemning partiality based on status, wealth, appearance. Treating people better because of what they can do for you or how they make you look. That's sinful favoritism. That's different from giving more responsibility to people who've earned trust through character and competence. That's not favoritism. That's stewardship. The question I have to ask myself is: Which one am I actually practicing?

The Questions I Need to Ask

When I look at my inner circle, the people I trust most and give the most opportunities to, I need to be honest about why they're there.

Question 1: Do my favorites get opportunities they've earned or opportunities they don't deserve?

This is the key distinction. Earned trust versus unearned preference. There are people on my team who've proven themselves over time. They deliver consistently. They show good judgment. They handle responsibility well. When I give them more opportunities, that's not favoritism, that's recognizing competence.

There are also people I just enjoy being around. People whose personalities mesh well with mine. People who laugh at my jokes, who think like I think, who make working together easier and more enjoyable. If I'm honest, I have to ask: Are those people getting opportunities because they've earned them through performance, or because I just like them?

If it's the former, that's wisdom. Matthew 25:14-30 (the Parable of the Talents) shows this principle: the servants who proved faithful with small things were given more. That's not favoritism, that's stewardship of responsibility. If it's the latter, if people are getting opportunities primarily because I enjoy working with them, that's a problem. That's showing partiality based on personal preference rather than proven character.

Question 2: Are my favorites truth-tellers or yes-men?

This is the test of whether my inner circle is actually helping me or just stroking my ego.

> **Proverbs 27:6** *"Faithful are the wounds of a friend; profuse are the kisses of an enemy."*

Real friends tell you hard truths. People who just tell you what you want to hear are not helping you, they're flattering you. If my inner circle is full of people who agree with everything I say, I haven't built a trust circle, I've built an echo chamber.

I have to ask: Do the people closest to me challenge me? Do they push back when they think I'm wrong? Do they bring perspectives I'm missing, or do they just affirm what I already think? If I've surrounded myself with people who make me feel smart and validated, that's not wisdom. That's insecurity disguised as leadership.

If the people I trust most are the ones who'll tell me when I'm missing something, when my plan has holes, when I'm making a mistake, that's a different kind of inner circle. That's iron sharpening iron (Proverbs 27:17).

Question 3: Does my inner circle reflect competence and character, or just comfort?

This is the hardest question because it requires me to evaluate my own motives. I like certain people. That's natural. Some personalities are easier for me to work with than others. Some people require less energy, less explanation, less friction.

Leadership isn't about surrounding myself with people who make my life easy. It's about surrounding myself with people who make the work better. There's a woman on my team who's excellent at her job. Detail-oriented, strategic thinker, delivers consistently, but she's also more direct than I'm naturally comfortable with. She'll challenge my ideas in ways that sometimes feel abrasive. Working with her requires more energy from me than working with people whose communication style matches mine.

I have to ask: Is she in my inner circle? Or have I subtly pushed her to the periphery because she's harder to work with, even though she's more valuable? If my inner circle is primarily people who are comfortable for me rather than people who are competent and have proven character, I've optimized for my own ease rather than the team's effectiveness. That's not leadership. That's self-indulgence.

The Pattern I'm Watching For

Here's what I'm learning to recognize in myself: favoritism isn't usually obvious. It's subtle. It shows up in small decisions that compound over time.

- Who do I ask for input first when a big decision needs to be made?

- Who gets invited to the strategic planning conversations?

- Who gets the high-visibility projects that can advance their careers?

- Who gets the benefit of the doubt when something goes wrong?

If the answer to all those questions is the same small group of people, and that group is defined more by who I like than by who's earned it, that's favoritism. If that group is defined by consistent performance, proven judgment, demonstrated character, and willingness to speak truth even when it's uncomfortable, that's an inner circle built on the right foundation.

The Biblical Caution

Even though Jesus, Paul, and David all had inner circles, that doesn't mean inner circles are automatically good. It depends entirely on what they're based on. David's inner circle of mighty men were there because they'd proven themselves in battle, demonstrated loyalty, and earned his trust (2 Samuel 23). That's the right kind of inner circle.

Later in his life, David's inner circle included Joab, who was competent but also ruthless and self-serving. Joab killed Absalom against David's explicit orders (2 Samuel 18:14). He murdered Abner and

Amasa to eliminate rivals (2 Samuel 3:27, 20:10). David kept Joab close because he was useful, not because he was trustworthy.

That's the wrong kind of inner circle. And it cost David dearly. One Psalm shows what David learned, probably too late:

> **Psalm 101:6-7** *"I will look with favor on the faithful in the land, that they may dwell with me; he who walks in the way that is blameless shall minister to me. No one who practices deceit shall dwell in my house; no one who utters lies shall continue before my eyes."*

The standard for the inner circle: faithfulness, blamelessness, honesty. Not just competence. Not just usefulness. Character. That's the standard I need to hold myself to when evaluating my own inner circle.

What I'm Learning to Do

I haven't figured this out. I still have favorites. I still give more time and attention to some people than others. And I still worry that I'm not being fair about it. I'm learning to audit my inner circle regularly. To ask hard questions about why certain people have access and others don't.

1. Regularly evaluate who has access and why

Every few months, I try to step back and ask: Who am I going to first for input? Who's getting the most significant opportunities and why? Is it because they've earned it through performance, or because I just like working with them?

If someone's in my inner circle primarily because they're easy to work with or because we get along well, that's a red flag. It doesn't mean I need to remove them, but it does mean I need to make sure I'm not overlooking other people who've earned access but don't have it because they're not as comfortable for me.

2. Intentionally seek diverse perspectives

If everyone in my inner circle thinks like me, I've built an echo chamber. That's dangerous. So I try to intentionally include people who see things differently. Who challenge my assumptions. Who bring perspectives I don't naturally have. That requires effort. It's easier to surround yourself with people who think like you. But it's not better.

> **Proverbs 15:22** *"Without counsel plans fail, but with many advisers they succeed."*

Many advisers. Not just the advisers who agree with me, but a genuine diversity of thought.

3. Make sure outsiders have a path to the inside

This is important: if my inner circle is a closed system where the same people get all the opportunities and no one new can earn their way in, that's not a trust circle. That's a clique.

I need to make sure there's a clear path for people to earn access. That high performance gets noticed. That character gets rewarded. That people who demonstrate competence and integrity can move from the periphery to the center. If the only way into my inner circle is to have been there from the beginning, I'm not building on merit. I'm building on familiarity. That's the wrong foundation.

4. Watch for the people I'm overlooking

This is the hardest one for me because I don't just have favorites. I also have people I've mentally sidelined. Not because they're incompetent. Not because they've failed. Sometimes just because they're harder to work with, or because their communication style doesn't match mine, or because they require more energy from me.

I have to ask: Am I overlooking someone who's actually excellent but just not comfortable for me?

The woman I mentioned earlier, the one who's more direct than I'm naturally comfortable with, she's someone I've had to consciously make sure I'm not sidelining just because she's harder to work with, because "harder to work with" often means "willing to challenge me," and that's actually valuable, not a liability.

The Hard Truth

I still mess this up. Regularly. There are people on my team who probably feel like they're on the outside looking in. They're probably right. Not because they haven't earned access, but because I've failed to give it to them. There are people I go to first, not because they're the best people for the job, but because they're the most comfortable for me to work with. There are people I've given opportunities to who maybe didn't fully earn them, just because I like them.

I'm trying to do better. I'm trying to base my inner circle on character and competence rather than comfort and compatibility, but it's a constant battle against my own natural preferences. That's the point of this chapter: acknowledging that having favorites isn't the problem. The problem is when favorites are based on the wrong things.

The Ongoing Work

1 Timothy 5:21 *"In the presence of God and of Christ Jesus and of the elect angels I charge you to keep these rules without prejudging, doing nothing from partiality."*

Do nothing from partiality. That's a high standard and it's one I fail at more often than I'd like to admit. The goal isn't perfection. The goal is faithfulness. Regularly examining my motives, honestly assessing my inner circle, making sure I'm building on the right foundation.

Jesus had an inner circle, but it was based on calling and purpose, not personal preference. Peter, James, and John weren't there because they made Jesus's life easier. They were there because they had roles to play in what He was building. Paul had an inner circle, but it was based on proven faithfulness and shared mission. Timothy got his focused mentorship because he'd demonstrated character and capability (Philippians 2:19-22). David's mighty men earned their place through loyalty and courage in battle. They weren't there because David liked them. They were there because they'd proven themselves.

That's the standard: earned trust, proven character, demonstrated competence, shared mission. Not comfort. Not compatibility. Not just because I like them. When I catch myself giving opportunities to people primarily because they're easy to work with, I need to stop and ask: Am I being a steward of these people and this organization, or am

I just optimizing for my own comfort? One is leadership. The other is self-indulgence.

The Secular Translation

If the Biblical framing doesn't resonate with you, here's the organizational behavior version: homogeneous teams underperform diverse teams.

When everyone in your inner circle thinks like you, comes from similar backgrounds, and has similar perspectives, you create blind spots. You miss problems you should see. You make decisions based on incomplete information because no one's bringing the perspective you're missing.

Research on diversity (cognitive diversity, not just demographic diversity) consistently shows that teams with diverse viewpoints make better decisions, catch more errors, and innovate more effectively than homogeneous teams. If your inner circle is defined by comfort rather than competence, you're optimizing for ease of communication at the expense of quality of decision-making.

The skill isn't avoiding favorites entirely. That's probably impossible and maybe not even desirable. The skill is ensuring that the people who get the most access and opportunity are there because they've earned it, not just because they make your life easier.

What I'm Still Learning

I don't have this figured out. I'm still working through this tension between having people I naturally trust more and making sure that trust is based on the right things.

Just last month, I caught myself giving a high-visibility project to someone in my inner circle when there was someone else on the team who was probably better suited for it. Not massively better, but better, and I had to ask myself: Am I giving this to the person I'm giving it to because they're the best choice, or because they're the comfortable choice?

The honest answer was: comfortable. They'd done similar projects before, I knew they'd deliver, it would require less oversight from me. So I made myself stop and reassess. I ended up giving the project to the other person, the one who was better suited but would require more of my time and energy to support.

It was the right call, but it required me to fight against my natural tendency to default to the people who make my life easiest. That's the ongoing work: recognizing when comfort is driving my decisions instead of stewardship.

The Long View

Proverbs 13:20 *"Whoever walks with the wise becomes wise, but the companion of fools will suffer harm."*

Who you surround yourself with matters. Your inner circle shapes you, for better or worse. If I surround myself with yes-men, I'll become arrogant. If I surround myself with people who only tell me what I want to hear, I'll become blind to my own failures.

If I surround myself with people who have proven character, who'll speak truth even when it's uncomfortable, who bring perspectives I'm missing, I'll become a better leader. The question isn't whether to have favorites. The question is what those favorites are based on. Are they based on character and competence or are they based on comfort and compatibility? Are they truth-tellers or yes-men? Do they challenge me or just affirm me? Have they earned access through performance and integrity, or do they have access because I just like them?

Those questions don't have easy answers and I don't always like what I find when I ask them honestly. That's the work of leadership: constantly evaluating yourself, auditing your own motives, making sure you're building on the right foundation. Not perfectly, but faithfully. Over time.

If you take nothing else from this chapter, take this: Having favorites isn't the problem. Favoritism is the problem.

There's a difference between giving more responsibility to people who've earned it through character and competence (stewardship) and giving more opportunity to people who just make your life easier (partiality). The first builds a strong organization. The second builds an echo chamber.

The only way to know which one you're building is to regularly, honestly, uncomfortably ask yourself: Why is this person in my inner circle and would they still be there if they challenged me more and comforted me less? If the answer to that second question is no, you don't have an inner circle built on trust. You have a clique built on preference. That will cost you more than you realize.

Part 5

Y ou've seen the framework built from pain. You've watched it
tested under pressure. You've learned how small decisions compound into culture. You've read the honest assessment of rough edges
still being sanded down. Now comes the question that matters most:
What does it mean to actually live this way?

Not just apply principles at work while compartmentalizing the
rest of your life. Not just lead well on Mondays while keeping your
faith confined to Sundays. Not just build a successful career while
treating your deepest convictions as private matters irrelevant to your
professional life, but actually integrated. One person. One framework.
One life where what you believe and how you lead aren't separate
things but the same thing expressed in different contexts.

This section brings it all together. What it looks like to stop compartmentalizing faith and work, to let Biblical truth shape everything
without being pushy or weird about it. How to be ready when people
ask why you lead differently, when your consistency creates enough
curiosity that they want to understand where it comes from. Why the
long view matters more than quarterly results, why building on rock
takes longer than building on sand, and why that's exactly why you
should do it.

For Christian leaders, this is about becoming the kind of person whose life raises questions your words can answer. For secular leaders, this is about building something that lasts beyond your tenure, creating influence that outlives your title, leading in a way that compounds over decades instead of just quarters.

This is where the atheist framework and the Biblical foundation converge. Where you see they were describing the same reality all along. Where truth proves itself by working, whether you acknowledge the source or not. Let me show you what integration actually looks like, and why it matters more than anything else in this book.

Chapter Sixteen

Beyond Sunday Morning

F or years, I lived in two worlds. There was Sunday Justin: the guy who went to church, studied Scripture, prayed, worshiped, tried to follow Jesus. That Justin cared about theology, spiritual growth, Biblical principles, and living a life that honored God.

Then there was Monday Justin: the CTO who had to deal with production outages, difficult clients, underperforming employees, and business decisions that didn't seem to have much to do with Sunday's sermon. That Justin cared about results, efficiency, profitability, and making sure the company didn't implode.

I didn't consciously decide to split myself in two. It just happened because the church world and the business world felt like they spoke different languages. One talked about grace and mercy and loving your neighbor. The other talked about accountability and performance and competitive advantage.

So I kept them separate. Faith lived in the "spiritual" bucket. Work lived in the "practical" bucket and I moved between them depending on which day of the week it was. I thought that's what everyone did. I thought that's what you were supposed to do. I was wrong.

The Problem With Compartmentalization

Here's what happens when you split your life into separate buckets: you become a different person depending on which context you're in.

That's not integration. That's fragmentation.

> **Romans 12:2** *"Do not be conformed to this world, but be transformed by the renewal of your mind, that by testing you may discern what is the will of God, what is good and acceptable and perfect."*

Transformed by the renewal of your mind. Not "transformed on Sundays." Not "spiritual in church contexts." Your *mind*, the way you think, the lens through which you see everything. I'd reduced faith to a set of behaviors I did in certain contexts. Pray before meals. Read the Bible in the morning. Be nice to people at church. Try not to sin too obviously.

Then I'd go to work and operate from a completely different framework: pragmatism, results, whatever gets the job done. I wasn't leading FROM Biblical conviction. I was leading from business pragmatism and occasionally adding some Jesus language on top when it seemed appropriate. That's not integration. That's compartmentalization with a spiritual veneer.

The Discovery That Changed Everything

Here's the thing that broke my compartmentalization: I didn't build
my leadership framework as a Christian exercise. I built it because I had
bad bosses who taught me what not to do. I built it through trial and
error over eighteen years, long before I was seriously following Jesus.
I built it because I wanted to lead well, not because I was trying to be
Biblical.

The four-part framework:

1. **Humility**: Who am I to judge? What am I missing?

2. **Whole Counsel**: What's the complete human and business
   impact?

3. **Restoration or Protection**: Can this be fixed, or does
   someone need defending?

4. **Moral Intuition**: Does this feel right based on principles,
   not politics?

I developed that framework in the marketplace, under pressure,
making real decisions with real consequences. It worked. Not perfectly, but consistently enough that I kept using it. Then, after I became
a Christian and started studying Scripture seriously, I kept seeing my
framework show up in the Bible.

1. **Humility?** That's all over Proverbs and the teachings of
   Jesus.

2. **Whole counsel?** That's seeing people as God sees them,
   considering their circumstances, understanding the whole
   picture.

3. **Restoration or protection?** That's the heart of the gospel
   and the purpose of leadership in the church.

4. **Moral intuition shaped by principles?** That's what it means to have your mind renewed by truth.

I hadn't been trying to build a Biblical framework. I'd been trying to build a *true* framework and it turned out those were the same thing.

Common Grace and Universal Truth

There's a theological concept called "common grace." It's the idea that God reveals truth to all people, not just Christians, through creation, conscience, and experience.

> **Psalm 19:1-2** "*The heavens declare the glory of God, and the sky above proclaims his handiwork. Day to day pours out speech, and night to night reveals knowledge.*"

Truth is accessible to anyone willing to look. You don't have to be a Christian to see that humility produces better decisions than arrogance. You don't have to believe in the Bible to recognize that grace often accomplishes more than punishment. You don't have to pray before making a decision to understand that considering whole counsel leads to wiser outcomes. Those principles work because they're *true*, not just because they're Christian.

Here's what that means for integration: I don't have to "bring Christianity to work" as if it's a foreign element I'm importing into a secular space. I just have to lead according to what's true. If I'm doing that, I'm leading Biblically whether I'm quoting Scripture or not.

The junior analyst I extended grace to? She never asked about my faith. She didn't need to. She experienced the fruit of Biblical principles in action. The framework worked for her benefit whether she knew it came from a Christian worldview or not. That's integration. Not making everything explicitly spiritual, but allowing Biblical truth to shape how I see people, how I make decisions, how I lead.

What Integration Actually Looks Like

Integration doesn't mean I pray before every business meeting (though sometimes I do). It doesn't mean I quote Scripture in presentations (I usually don't). It doesn't mean I try to evangelize my team during standup meetings (that would be weird and inappropriate). Integration means my faith shapes my operating system, not just my vocabulary.

> **Colossians 3:23** *"Whatever you do, work heartily, as for the Lord and not for men."*

Whatever you do. Not "whatever spiritual work you do." Not "when you're at church." *Whatever you do.* That includes code reviews. Client meetings. Performance evaluations. Budget decisions. Hiring. Firing. All of it. The question isn't "How do I make this more Christian?" The question is "How do I do this in a way that reflects what's true about people, leadership, justice, mercy, and wisdom?"

When I extended grace to the QA analyst, I wasn't thinking, "I need to be Christian about this." I was thinking, "I've made this mistake before, this person deserves restoration, destroying her life over an honest error violates something fundamental about how people should be treated." That's Biblical thinking. I just didn't label it that way in the moment.

The Difference Between Preaching and Living

Here's what I've learned: people don't need me to preach at them. They need me to lead well. A verse in 1 Peter often quoted as a mandate to evangelize, but notice what it actually says:

> **1 Peter 3:15** *"In your hearts honor Christ the Lord as holy, always being prepared to make a defense for the hope that is in you; yet do it with gentleness and respect."*

There's an order here:

1. Honor Christ in your heart (internal conviction)

2. Live in a way that makes people curious about that conviction

3. Be prepared to explain when they ask

4. Do it with gentleness and respect, not pushiness

The sequence matters. You don't start by explaining your faith. You start by *living* your faith in a way that makes people want to understand where it comes from.

The women who reported harassment to me didn't need to know I was a Christian (some did) to trust me. They needed to see that I protected vulnerable people, that I kept confidence, that I valued integrity over politics. They experienced the fruit of Biblical leadership before they knew the root. That's more powerful than any sermon I could have given them.

When Faith Shapes How You See

The biggest shift in integration for me wasn't adding more Jesus language to my vocabulary. It was allowing Biblical truth to change how I see people and situations. When I look at an underperforming employee, do I see a liability to be managed or a person made in God's image who might be struggling?

When I'm making a decision that affects people's livelihoods, do I see it as a business calculation or as stewardship of responsibility God has entrusted to me? When someone fails, do I see it as a problem to be punished or as an opportunity for restoration?

> **Romans 12:2** "...transformed by the renewal of your mind."

That transformation isn't about thinking more religious thoughts. It's about seeing reality differently. When I see an employee who's made a costly mistake, I don't just see a liability to be managed. I see a whole person, made in God's image, deserving of dignity even in failure, capable of redemption. When I face a decision that affects someone's livelihood, I don't just see a business calculation. I see stewardship of responsibility God has entrusted to me.

That Biblical lens doesn't make the decisions easier, but it does make them clearer. It roots them in something deeper than pragmatism or quarterly results. That's what integration actually means: your faith changes the lens through which you see everything, not just "spiritual" things.

The Tension With Secular Environments

I know what some of you are thinking: "That's great for you, but I work in a secular environment. I can't talk about God. I can't quote the Bible. I have to keep my faith private or I'll be seen as unprofessional or even create legal problems." I get it and I'm not suggesting you violate workplace policies or make people uncomfortable by being preachy.

Here's the thing: you don't have to talk about your faith to lead from it. When you extend grace to someone who fails, you're living out the gospel whether you mention Jesus or not. When you protect someone vulnerable, you're reflecting God's heart for justice whether you quote Scripture or not. When you tell the truth even when it costs you, you're demonstrating Biblical integrity whether you frame it religiously or not.

The secular world doesn't need more Christian jargon. It needs more people who actually live according to what's true. If you're doing that, you're being a witness to Biblical principles even if you never use Biblical language. People notice when you lead differently. When you treat people with dignity they're not used to receiving. When you make decisions based on principle instead of politics. When you extend grace instead of judgment.

When they notice, some of them will ask. Not "Are you a Christian?" necessarily, but "Why do you lead like that?" "Where does that come from?" "How do you stay calm under pressure?" Those questions create openings and when those openings come, you can explain. With gentleness and respect. Without being pushy or preachy. The opening comes from living it first, not from talking about it first.

What Changed for Me

The shift from compartmentalization to integration didn't happen overnight. It was gradual. Here's what changed:

I stopped asking "What's the Christian thing to do?"

That question assumes there's a spiritual answer and a practical answer, and you have to choose between them. Instead, I started asking "What's the *true* thing to do?" What's true about this person? What's true about this situation? What's true about how people grow, how trust is built, how justice and mercy should intersect? When I asked those questions, I found that the true thing and the Biblical thing were the same thing.

I stopped separating "spiritual" and "practical"

I used to think some decisions were spiritual (how to handle moral failures, how to treat people) and some were practical (how to structure teams, what technology to use, budget allocations). If God cares about truth, justice, wisdom, and stewardship, then *all* decisions have a spiritual dimension. Not because they're explicitly religious, but because they involve principles God cares about.

How I structure a team affects how people flourish or suffer. That's not just organizational design, that's stewardship of people God made. What technology I choose affects whether we're being good stewards of resources or wasteful. That's not just technical, that's about wisdom and stewardship. Budget decisions affect people's livelihoods, the company's health, and whether we're living within our means. That's not just finance, that's about justice and integrity.

Everything is spiritual if you see it rightly. Not because you're always praying about it, but because everything involves principles God cares about.

I started seeing my work as worship

Colossians 3:23 "work heartily, as for the Lord."

That's not just about working hard. It's about recognizing that your work *matters* to God. Not because it's religious work, but because it's human flourishing, stewardship, justice, mercy, truth, all things God cares about deeply.

When I write good code, that's not just craftsmanship. That's stewarding the abilities God gave me. When I make a wise hiring decision, that's not just HR. That's helping someone flourish in work God designed humans to do. When I lead well, that's not just management. That's reflecting, however imperfectly, the kind of leadership God demonstrates.

I don't have to make it explicitly Christian for it to be worship. I just have to do it as unto the Lord, recognizing that He cares about it even if no one at work knows that's why I care about it.

The Freedom This Brings

Here's what surprised me about integration: it's freeing. When I was compartmentalizing, I was constantly managing which version of me I needed to be in which context. I had to remember what I could say and couldn't say, what principles applied in which bucket, how to be

"Christian enough" in church settings and "professional enough" in work settings. It was exhausting.

When I stopped compartmentalizing, when I just let Biblical truth shape how I saw everything, I could be the same person everywhere. Not perfectly, but consistently. I didn't have to code-switch. I didn't have to remember which Justin to be. I could just lead according to what's true, and trust that truth would serve people well whether they knew it came from Scripture or not.

> **Matthew 6:33** *"But seek first the kingdom of God and his righteousness, and all these things will be added to you."*

When I sought to lead according to what's true and right, the "Christian" part and the "professional" part stopped being in tension. They became integrated. Righteousness isn't just spiritual, it's about doing what's right in every context. Doing what's right benefits everyone, whether they share your faith or not.

The Test of Integration

Here's how you know if you've actually integrated your faith into your work: Would your leadership change if you stopped being a Christian? If the answer is "not really, I'd still lead basically the same way," then your faith isn't actually integrated. It's just a label you put on behavior you'd have anyway. If the answer is "absolutely, my entire framework would collapse without the Biblical foundation," then you've integrated.

For me, the answer is the latter. Without the Biblical understanding of human dignity, grace, justice, restoration, and truth, my framework falls apart. I wouldn't know *why* I should extend grace to the junior analyst instead of firing her. I wouldn't know *why* I should protect vulnerable people at cost to myself. I wouldn't know *why* truth matters more than winning.

My framework isn't just informed by Scripture. It's *dependent* on Scripture. On the truth Scripture reveals about who people are, how they change, what justice requires, how grace works. Take that foundation away, and I don't have a leadership philosophy. I just have a collection of preferences.

For Christian Leaders: Stop Splitting Yourself

If you're a Christian leader who's been compartmentalizing, here's my challenge: stop. Stop having "spiritual you" and "work you." Stop thinking some decisions are Biblical and some are just practical. Stop trying to add Jesus language on top of decisions you're making for purely pragmatic reasons.

Let Biblical truth shape how you see *everything*. Let your faith inform your operating system, not just your religious vocabulary. You don't have to quote the Bible in every meeting. You don't have to pray out loud before every decision. You don't have to make everything explicitly Christian. You just have to let the truth of Scripture shape how you think, how you see people, how you make decisions. Then lead according to that truth. Consistently. Whether people know it's Biblical or not.

The fruit of Biblical leadership will be evident even if the roots aren't visible. For many of the people you lead, experiencing that fruit will be far more powerful than hearing the theology behind it.

For Secular Leaders: These Principles Are True

If you're not a Christian, you might be thinking, "This is all well and good for you, but it doesn't apply to me." Actually, it does. The principles I've been describing aren't true because they're Christian. They're Christian because they're true.

Humility produces better decisions than arrogance, regardless of your theology. Understanding whole counsel leads to wiser outcomes than snap judgments, whether you pray about it or not. Grace often accomplishes more than punishment, even if you don't believe in the gospel. Integrity builds trust and lies destroy it, regardless of what Scripture says about it.

These principles work because they align with reality. They're descriptions of how people actually function, how trust is actually built, how change actually happens. I'm not asking you to become a Christian. I'm just asking you to consider whether there might be wisdom in principles that have been tested for 3,000 years and keep showing up because they're true.

You can lead according to these principles without sharing my faith. You'll just be leading according to what's true. If you do that consistently, you'll probably find that it works better than the alternatives.

The Long View

Integration is a journey, not a destination. I haven't arrived. There are still areas where I default to compartmentalization, where I slip into "practical" mode and forget that all of life is spiritual if I'm seeing it rightly. I'm further along than I was, and the more I integrate, the more free I become. The more consistent I become. The more effective I become.

Not because I'm more religious, but because I'm more aligned. The same truth that shapes my Sunday is shaping my Monday. That consistency, over time, builds something that fragmentation never could. **James 1:8** describes a double-minded man as "unstable in all his ways." That was me for years. Spiritual on Sunday, pragmatic on Monday. Unstable because I was trying to operate from two different foundations.

When faith shapes everything, when truth is the lens through which you see all of life, you become stable. Not perfect, but consistent. That consistency builds trust, credibility, and effectiveness over time. If you take nothing else from this chapter, take this: Stop compartmentalizing. Your faith isn't just for Sunday morning. It's for Monday's production crisis, Tuesday's difficult client meeting, Wednesday's performance review, Thursday's budget decision, and Friday's moral dilemma.

Let Biblical truth shape how you see everything. Not by making everything explicitly religious, but by allowing what's true to inform how you think, decide, and lead. The world doesn't need more Christian leaders who are spiritual on Sunday and pragmatic the rest of the week. It needs leaders who've been transformed by truth, who see people and situations through a lens shaped by what's actually real and right, and who lead accordingly. Whether they use Biblical language or not. That's integration and it changes everything.

Chapter Seventeen

When They Ask

I 've never led a Bible study at work (I have led prayer with a small
group). I've never put Scripture verses in my email signature. I
don't have a Jesus fish on my laptop or a cross on my desk. I'm not
hiding my faith. If someone asks, I'll tell them, but I'm not advertising
it either.

I learned early on that the worst kind of evangelism is the pushy
kind. The kind that makes people uncomfortable. The kind where
you're so eager to talk about your faith that you turn every conversation into an opportunity to preach, whether people want to hear it
or not.

I've seen that approach backfire more times than I can count. People tune out. They avoid you. They put you in the "religious weirdo"
category and stop taking you seriously. I've also seen the opposite
approach work powerfully. Not hiding your faith, but not forcing it
either. Just living in a way that makes people curious. When they get
curious enough to ask, be ready with an answer.

That's what this chapter is about: the conversations that happen
when you lead well enough, long enough, that people start wondering
why you lead the way you do.

The Order That Matters

A verse is 1 Peter is probably the most misquoted verse about evangelism:

> **1 Peter 3:15** *"But in your hearts honor Christ the Lord as holy, always being prepared to make a defense for the hope that is in you; yet do it with gentleness and respect."*

Most people focus on the "always being prepared" part. That's important, but notice what comes before it: *for the hope that is in you.* Not "the theological position you hold" or "the doctrine you believe." The *hope that is in you.* Something visible enough, different enough, compelling enough that people want to understand where it comes from.

Notice the context: you're making a defense. That means someone is asking. Someone is questioning. Someone has noticed something about you that made them curious. The order matters:

1. **Live** with such integrity and hope that people notice something different

2. **Wait** for them to ask about it

3. **Explain** with gentleness and respect when they do

Most Christians get this backwards. They start with explaining, hoping that their words will convince people. 1 Peter 3:15 assumes your life has already raised the question. Your words are just the answer to a question your behavior prompted. If no one's asking, you're probably not living in a way that creates curiosity.

When No One's Asking

For the first few months I was a Christian, I don't think anyone at work noticed. Not because I was hiding it, but because my leadership didn't look any different than it did before I came to faith. I still led from the same pragmatic, results-driven playbook I always had. I just happened to also go to church on Sundays.

I was compartmentalized, like I talked about in the last chapter and compartmentalized faith doesn't create curiosity. It just makes you religious in private and normal in public. As I started integrating my faith, as Biblical truth started shaping how I actually led, not just what I believed, people started noticing. Not in a "you're acting weird" way. In a "you handle things differently" way.

The junior analyst who deleted production data expected to be fired. When I extended grace instead, it stood out. Not because I quoted Scripture, but because the response didn't match what she expected from a typical CTO. The women who reported harassment had watched me for months, noticing how I treated people with dignity regardless of rank, how I kept confidence, how I protected vulnerable people. That pattern created trust. Eventually, it created questions.

Not "Are you a Christian?" initially. But "Why do you lead like that?" "Where does that come from?" "How do you stay so calm when everything's falling apart?" Those questions opened the door.

The Conversations That Followed

I remember one specific conversation with a senior developer on my team, let's call him David. We'd been working together for several months. He'd watched me handle several crises, make hard decisions, extend grace when he expected judgment. We were on a call one day, post-crisis, something we'd just successfully navigated and he said, almost offhand, "You know, you handle pressure differently than any other leader I've worked for. Where does that come from?"

That's the question. Not "Are you religious?" but "Where does *that* come from?" I could have deflected. Could have said something generic like "Oh, I just try to stay calm" or "Experience, I guess", but he was asking. Genuinely. 1 Peter 3:15 says be ready to give an answer. So I told him: "Honestly, a lot of it comes from my faith. I'm a Christian, and the way I think about people, about failure, about grace, that's shaped by how I understand the gospel."

Notice what I didn't do: I didn't launch into a sermon. I didn't ask him if he was saved. I didn't try to convince him he needed Jesus. I just answered his question. Honestly, directly, and left space for him to respond. His response: "Huh. I wouldn't have guessed that. You don't seem like most Christians I've met."

I took that as a compliment because most Christians he'd met probably compartmentalized their faith or pushed it on people. He'd never seen integrated faith that showed up in leadership without being pushy about it. We talked for another twenty minutes. He had questions. I answered them. Some theological, some practical. "How does Christianity shape how you make decisions?" "Do you think non-Christians can lead well?" "What do you do when faith and business seem to conflict?"

I didn't have perfect answers to all of them, but I was honest, and I didn't try to convert him. I just explained, as clearly as I could, how my faith shaped my framework. That conversation didn't end with him becoming a Christian. It did change how he saw Christianity. It made it real instead of theoretical. Practical instead of abstract. That's what 1 Peter 3:15 is after: not conversion in the moment, but an honest, respectful explanation of where your hope comes from. Our role is not to grow the seeds of faith. Our role is to plant them and let God go to work!

What to Actually Say

When people ask about your faith, especially in a work context, there are a few things I've learned to do and not do.

Do: Connect it to what they've observed

Don't start with theology. Start with what they've noticed. If they're asking because you handled a difficult situation with grace, connect your faith to that: "The way I think about failure and restoration comes from how I understand the gospel. God extended grace to me when I didn't deserve it, and that shapes how I think about extending grace to others."

If they're asking because you stayed calm under pressure, connect it there: "My faith gives me a longer view. I believe God is sovereign over outcomes, which means I can do my best and trust that the results aren't ultimately in my control. That takes some of the pressure off." Start with the concrete thing they observed, then connect it to the theological foundation. That makes it real instead of abstract.

Don't: Turn it into a salvation presentation

This is a work conversation, not an evangelistic crusade. You're not trying to get them to pray the sinner's prayer in the conference room. You're just explaining where your leadership framework comes from. How your faith shapes your decision-making. Why you operate the way you do.

If they want to know more about Christianity generally, they'll ask, and you can have that conversation. But don't force it. The goal isn't conversion in the moment. The goal is planting seeds, showing them that faith can be integrated and practical, not just theoretical and religious.

Do: Be honest about struggles

Don't present yourself as having it all figured out. That's not honest, and it's not helpful. When I talk about how my faith shapes my leadership, I also talk about where I struggle. The tension between grace and accountability. The times I've failed to live up to my own principles. The ongoing work of becoming the leader I want to be.

> **Philippians 3:12** *"Not that I have already obtained this or am already perfect, but I press on to make it my own, because Christ Jesus has made me his own."*

You're not selling perfection. You're explaining a framework that's shaping you, even though you're still being shaped. That honesty makes you credible because everyone knows you're not perfect. If you pretend you are, they'll dismiss everything you say as religious posturing.

Don't: Get defensive or preachy

Some people will ask genuine questions. Others will push back, maybe even challenge your faith. When that happens, don't get defensive. Don't try to win the argument. Don't shift into "let me prove Christianity to you" mode. 1 Peter 3:15 says do it with "gentleness and respect." That means treating their questions as legitimate, even if you disagree with their premises. It means being confident in your faith without being arrogant about it.

If they say something like "I don't see how you can be a rational person and believe in God," you don't have to defend the entire theological enterprise of Christianity. You can just say, "I understand why you see it that way. For me, faith and reason aren't in conflict. But I respect that you see it differently." Sometimes I'll talk about how I was an athiest not to long ago so I understand their doubt.

You're not conceding your faith. You're just acknowledging that reasonable people can disagree. That's actually more powerful than trying to argue them into believing.

Do: Invite further conversation if they want it

If they seem genuinely interested, let them know you're open to talking more. "If you ever want to talk more about this, I'm happy to. No pressure, but I enjoy these conversations." That leaves the door open without being pushy. They can follow up if they want. Or not. Either way, you've been faithful to answer when asked, without forcing it on them.

The Questions I've Gotten

Over the years, here are some of the actual questions people have asked me when they've been curious about my faith:

"Do you really believe the Bible is true?"

My answer: "I do. Completely, and I say that as someone who didn't for a long time.

Talking donkeys? Come on. A guy living in a whale? Please. Six-day creation? I had the same reaction most educated people have: 'Yeah, some good wisdom in there, but let's not take it *literally*.' Here's what changed: I actually read it. Not skimming for inspirational quotes. Not cherry-picking the parts that felt safe. I read the whole thing with an open heart, willing to be wrong about what I thought I knew.

I realized *I* was the problem, not the text. I'd been dismissing it from a position of arrogance. I had decided ahead of time what God could and couldn't do, what was 'reasonable' for Him to allow or accomplish. Once I stopped trying to edit God down to what made sense to me, the whole thing came into focus. Yes, I believe Balaam's donkey spoke. Yes, I believe Jonah survived in that fish. Yes, I believe God created everything. Not because I abandoned my brain, but because I stopped pretending my brain was big enough to tell God what's possible.

The Bible is God's revelation of truth. All of it. I've found that when I take it seriously, even the parts that sound impossible, it proves itself true in how I actually live and lead."

"How do you reconcile faith with logic and science?"

My answer: "For me, they're not in conflict. I see science as describing *how* things work, and faith as addressing *why* things exist and what they mean. I don't think you have to choose between being rational and being a believer. The more science evolves the more evident it becomes that Science and faith are ultimately coming to the same conclusion."

That's not a full apologetic, but it's enough to show I'm not anti-intellectual, and it doesn't require a thirty-minute lecture on epistemology.

"How does being a Christian affect how you do your job?"

This is the best question, because it's what they've already observed and are trying to understand.

My answer: "It shapes how I see people, mostly. I believe everyone is made in God's image, which means everyone has inherent dignity and worth. That affects how I handle failure, how I make decisions about people's careers, how I think about justice and mercy. It's not a separate thing I do at work, it's the lens through which I see everything." That connects faith directly to leadership in a way that's practical, not preachy.

"Why don't you talk about your faith more?"

This one surprised me the first time I got it, but it's a fair question.

My answer: "Because I don't want to be pushy or make people uncomfortable. I'd rather people see my faith in how I lead than hear me talk about it constantly, but I'm always happy to talk about it if people are curious." That clarifies that silence isn't hiding, it's respecting boundaries, and it affirms that I'm open to the conversation when they want to have it.

When the Conversation Gets Deeper

Sometimes, the conversation doesn't stop at surface questions. Some-times people want to know more. They're genuinely wrestling with spiritual questions, and your leadership has created enough credibility that they trust you to engage honestly.

When that happens, here's what I try to do:

Listen more than talk

Most people who are wrestling with faith questions aren't looking for a lecture. They're looking for someone who will actually listen to their doubts, their objections, their confusion.

So I ask questions: "What's making you think about this?" "Where are you wrestling?" "What's holding you back from faith?"

Then I listen. Really listen. Not formulating my response while they're talking, but actually hearing what they're saying.

Acknowledge legitimate doubts

Some of the objections people have to Christianity are legitimate. Suffering. Hypocrisy in the church. Intellectual questions about the resurrection or the problem of evil.

I don't pretend those aren't real issues. I acknowledge them: "Yeah, that's a hard question. I've wrestled with that too. Here's how I think about it, but I don't claim to have a perfect answer." That honesty builds trust, because they know you're not just giving them canned answers, you're engaging with the real questions.

Point to Jesus, not religion

A lot of people's objections to Christianity are actually objections to religious behavior, not to Jesus Himself.

So when possible, I try to distinguish between the two: "Yeah, the church has done a lot of damage. I get why that's a stumbling block, but can I ask, what do you think about Jesus Himself? Not Christians generally, but Jesus?" That shifts the conversation from religion (which they may have legitimate reasons to reject) to the person of Jesus (who's much harder to dismiss if you actually look at what He said and did).

Offer resources if they want them

If someone is genuinely interested in exploring faith further, I'll offer resources. Books that helped me. Podcasts. People they could talk to. I don't force it. I just say, "If you're interested in reading more about this, I'd recommend X. But no pressure."

If they are open to reading the Bible I recommend they start in the New Testament. Matthew, maybe James or John. One of the Gospel books that truly define who Jesus was and is. The goal is to facilitate their journey, not control it.

The Conversations That Don't Happen

Here's the reality: most people won't ask. Not because you're doing anything wrong. Just because they're not curious, or they're not ready, or they've got their own framework and aren't looking for a new one, and that's okay. Your job isn't to force conversations. It's to live in a way that's worth asking about. And if no one asks, you're still being faithful.

> **Matthew 5:16** *"Let your light shine before others, so that they may see your good works and give glory to your Father who is in heaven."*

Notice: *they* may give glory. Not "you convince them to give glory" or "you preach at them until they give glory." You shine, they see, and if they respond by glorifying God, that's their response to what they've seen. You can't control whether they ask. You can only control whether your life is worth asking about.

The Balance I'm Still Learning

I don't have this perfectly figured out. There are times when I've been too quiet, missed opportunities to explain my faith when someone genuinely wanted to hear. There are other times when I've been too eager, pushed a conversation further than it needed to go, made someone uncomfortable by being too explicit about my faith too soon.

The balance is hard: not hiding, but not forcing. Being open without being pushy. Ready to explain without being preachy. I'm learning and here's what I'm learning toward: trust the process. Live well. Lead according to truth. Let your character create curiosity. When people ask, answer honestly, with gentleness and respect. That's 1 Peter 3:15 in practice, and it's more powerful than any evangelistic strategy I could manufacture.

For Christian Leaders: Be Worth Asking About

If you're a Christian leader and no one's ever asked you about your faith, that should prompt some self-reflection. Not guilt. Not shame. Just honest assessment: Is my leadership different enough, compelling enough, that it raises questions? Am I leading the same way everyone else does, just with a Jesus bumper sticker on my personal life? Integration creates curiosity. Compartmentalization doesn't.

If your faith is shaping how you actually lead, people will notice. Some of them will ask. Not everyone, but some. When they do, be ready. Not with a sermon, but with an honest explanation of where your framework comes from. That's faithful witness. It's far more effective than trying to force spiritual conversations into contexts where they don't fit.

For Secular Leaders: Why This Matters

If you're not a Christian, you might be wondering why this chapter is relevant to you.

Here's why: even if you don't share my faith, you probably have principles that shape your leadership. Values that inform your decisions. A framework that guides how you treat people. If you lead well according to those principles, people will notice. They'll ask where it comes from. You should be ready to explain.

Not to convert them to your worldview, but to help them understand why you lead the way you do. To show them that leadership isn't just about tactics, it's about principles. That those principles come from somewhere. Whether your framework is shaped by Stoicism, humanism, Eastern philosophy, or just hard-won experience, if it's producing good leadership, it's worth explaining when people ask.

People are looking for leaders who operate from conviction, not just convenience. Who have a framework, not just a playbook. Who can explain *why* they do what they do, not just *what* they do. That depth creates influence. Influence creates opportunities to shape how others lead, which multiplies your impact far beyond your direct reports.

The Long View

I don't know how many people have become Christians because of conversations that started with them asking about my leadership. Maybe none. Maybe some. That's not really mine to track. What I do know is that I've had dozens of conversations where people engaged with Christianity in a real way, maybe for the first time, because they'd seen it lived out in a context that mattered to them.

Not church. Not a Bible study. Not a theological debate. Work. Leadership. Real decisions under real pressure. That made it real. Made it worth considering. Made it something other than abstract religious theory. That's what 1 Peter 3:15 is after. Not conversion quotas. Just faithful witness. Living in a way that creates curiosity, and being ready to explain when people are curious enough to ask.

With gentleness. With respect. Without being pushy or preachy. Just honest conversation about where your hope comes from. If you take nothing else from this chapter, take this: Don't force spiritual conversations, but don't avoid them either. Live well enough, long enough, that your leadership raises questions.

When people ask, answer honestly. Not with a sermon. Not with a sales pitch. Just an honest explanation of where your framework comes from and how it shapes the way you lead. That's faithful witness. Over time, it's far more powerful than any evangelistic strategy you could manufacture.

It's rooted in reality, not theory. In transformation, not information. In a life that's worth asking about, not just words you want people to hear. That's what the world needs: fewer Christians who talk about faith and more Christians who live it in a way that makes people want to understand where it comes from. Be the latter and be ready when they ask.

Chapter Eighteen

The Long View

E very quarter, I get the same question from leadership: "What are the numbers?" Revenue. Profit margins. Burn rate. Client acquisition. Retention metrics. All the short-term indicators that tell you whether this quarter was better or worse than last quarter. Those things matter. I'm not dismissing them. You can't run a business by ignoring financial reality. Bills have to be paid. Investors have to see returns. Clients have to be satisfied.

Here's the tension: corporate America operates on 90-day cycles. Quarterly earnings calls. Quarterly reviews. Quarterly pressure to show growth, improvement, progress that can be measured and reported. Leadership decisions made under that kind of pressure tend to optimize for the short term. Quick wins. Immediate results. Whatever makes this quarter look better than last quarter.

The principles I've been writing about in this book, they don't work on 90-day timelines. They work on years-long timelines. Sometimes decades-long. Grace doesn't show immediate ROI. Trust compounds slowly. Character is built over time, not quarters. Building a culture that actually lasts, that requires the long view. Which means leading Biblically often puts you at odds with the corporate pressure to deliver quarterly results.

The Corporate Pressure

I've been in countless meetings where the conversation goes like this:

"We need to hit this revenue target. What are we going to do to close the gap?"

Inevitably, someone proposes something that will work short-term but damage things long-term.

"Let's commit to features we know we can't deliver by the timeline the client wants. We'll figure it out later."

"Let's cut that employee now to make the numbers work, even though we'll need them in six months."

"Let's push this product to market even though it's not ready. We can fix the bugs in production."

These aren't hypothetical. I've heard all of them. The pressure behind them is real. Miss your quarterly targets enough times and investors lose confidence. Miss them badly enough and you lose your job. So the temptation is always there: sacrifice long-term health for short-term survival. Sometimes, you have to make hard short-term decisions to ensure there is a long term. I'm not suggesting you ignore financial reality in the name of idealism.

There's a difference between making hard decisions to survive and making dishonest decisions to hit arbitrary targets. The first is stewardship. The second is building on sand.

The Biblical Alternative

The Bible operates on a completely different timeline than quarterly earnings.

Proverbs 13:22 *"A good man leaves an inheritance to his children's children."*

Not "a good man hits his quarterly targets." Not "a good man maximizes shareholder value this year." An inheritance to his children's children. That's a multi-generational view. That's building something that outlasts you. That's the long view.

Matthew 7:24-27 *"Everyone then who hears these words of mine and does them will be like a wise man who built his house on the rock. And the rain fell, and the floods came, and the winds blew and beat on that house, but it did not fall, because it had been founded on the rock. And everyone who hears these words of mine and does not do them will be like a foolish man who built his house on the sand. And the rain fell, and the floods came, and the winds blew and beat against that house, and it fell, and great was the fall of it."*

Both builders experienced the same storms. Both faced the same pressure. The difference wasn't the external circumstances. It was what they'd built on. Rock takes longer to build on. It's harder. It requires more work up front, but when the storm comes, it holds.

Sand is easier. Faster. You can build something impressive-looking on sand in a fraction of the time, but when the storm comes, it collapses. That's the tension: do you build for quarterly results (sand), or do you build on principles that hold when pressure comes (rock)?

The Examples From Earlier Chapters

Every major decision I've written about in this book involved this tension between short-term pressure and long-term principle.

The Junior Analyst: Short-Term Cost, Long-Term Gain

When the junior analyst deleted production data, the short-term answer was obvious: fire her. Send a message. Make an example. Show everyone that costly mistakes have consequences. That would have been the quick win. Decisive action. Immediate response. The kind of thing you can report in a quarterly review: "Addressed performance issue swiftly and decisively."

I took the long view. I extended grace. Invested in restoration. Accepted the short-term cost of keeping an employee who'd made a massive mistake. Long-term? She became one of my most loyal employees. She survived the first round of layoffs because of that loyalty, and when we had to let her go in the second round, we went to war for her because the relationship we'd built was worth fighting for.

The short-term cost was real, but the long-term gain was greater. If I'd optimized for the quarter, I'd have fired her. If I'd optimized for the long-term principle (people are worth investing in, grace builds loyalty), I kept her. I'm glad I took the long view.

The Sales Meeting: Quick Win vs. Lasting Relationship

When the salesman started lying about features our AI product didn't have, I could have stayed quiet. We might have closed the deal that day. Signed the contract. Hit our revenue target for the quarter. Everyone would have been happy, short-term.

Then, six months later, the client would have discovered we couldn't deliver what was promised. The relationship would have imploded. We'd have lost them as a client, probably faced legal consequences, and destroyed our reputation in the process. We would have been like every other vendor they had worked with.

That's a long-term problem, and when you're under pressure to hit quarterly numbers, long-term problems feel distant and theoretical. I chose the long view. I corrected the lies in the moment, even though it risked losing the deal immediately.

Short-term, it was painful. I had to eat crow in front of the client. The salesman was furious with me. We almost lost the opportunity.

Long-term? They became one of our largest clients. Not because we promised them the moon, but because we told them the truth. The relationship was built on realistic expectations and trust, not on lies that would eventually collapse.

If I'd optimized for the quarter, I'd have let the lies stand and dealt with the consequences later. If I'd optimized for the long-term principle (truth builds trust, lies build collapse), I spoke up. I'm glad I took the long view.

The Billing Mistake: The Cover-Up That Destroyed Everything

This is the painful one. The time I didn't take the long view. The time I let short-term pressure override long-term principle. We'd accidentally billed a client $350,000 more than we should have. They didn't notice. The following month, our accounting team discovered the error.

The CFO and CEO wanted to keep it and I went along with it. Not because I thought it was right, but because refunding it meant laying off two people on my team. That was the short-term calculation: keep the money, save the jobs, everyone's happy. Except three months later, they discovered it anyway. We had to refund the money, AND we lost them as a client because we'd broken their trust.

The thing I was trying to protect (jobs, revenue, client relationship) got destroyed by the cover-up. The short-term gain cost us everything long-term. If I'd taken the long view from the beginning, I'd have refunded the money immediately, been honest about the mistake, and trusted that honesty would preserve the relationship even if it cost us in the moment.

Instead, I optimized for the short term and it cost us everything the short-term thinking was supposed to protect. That's what happens when you build on sand instead of rock. It might look fine for a while, but when the storm comes, it collapses.

The Pattern: Principles Hold, Pressure Doesn't

Here's what I've learned from these and dozens of other decisions: principles hold under pressure. Short-term thinking collapses under pressure. When you make decisions based on long-term principles (grace, truth, integrity, trust), you might take short-term hits. But over time, those principles compound. They build something that lasts.

When you make decisions based on short-term pressure (hit this number, avoid this pain, protect this quarter), you might get immediate results. Over time, those decisions undermine the foundation you're trying to build.

Galatians 6:7-9 *"Do not be deceived: God is not mocked, for whatever one sows, that will he also reap. For the one who sows to his own flesh will from the flesh reap corruption, but the one who sows to the Spirit will from the Spirit reap eternal life. And let us not grow weary of doing good, for in due season we will reap, if we do not give up."*

You reap what you sow. Not immediately. *In due season.* If you sow short-term thinking, you'll reap long-term collapse. Maybe not this quarter, maybe not this year, but eventually. If you sow long-term principles, you'll reap lasting fruit. Maybe not this quarter, maybe not this year, but *in due season.* The question is: which timeline are you building for?

The Temptation to Compromise

The hardest part about taking the long view is that the pressure to compromise is constant. Every quarter, there's a new crisis. A new target to hit. A new reason why this time you need to make an exception to your principles.

- "I know we said we'd always tell the truth, but this one time, we really need this deal."

- "I know we said we'd treat people with dignity, but we have to make cuts and we can't afford to be soft."

- "I know we said we'd build on principle, but the investors are breathing down our necks and we need results *now.*"

The pressure is real and I'm not dismissing it. Sometimes you're in survival mode and you have to make hard decisions quickly. Here's the question I've learned to ask: Is this decision moving me toward the foundation I want to build on, or away from it? Am I making a hard decision that's still consistent with my principles, or am I compromising my principles because the pressure is too great?

The first might be painful, but it's still building on rock. The second might relieve immediate pressure, but it's building on sand. When the next storm comes, which foundation do I want to be standing on?

Building Culture That Outlasts You

Here's the other thing about the long view: you're not just building a career. You're building a culture. The decisions you make today shape the environment your team will operate in long after you're gone. The principles you model become the norms they adopt. The compromises you make become the precedents they follow.

When I extended grace to the junior analyst, I wasn't just making a decision about her. I was establishing a cultural norm: we value people over performance metrics. We believe in restoration over punishment. We extend grace when people fail honestly. That culture outlasted my time with that company. People who were watching that decision remembered it. When they became leaders themselves, some of them led the same way. Not because I told them to, but because they'd seen it modeled.

When I corrected the lies in the sales meeting, I wasn't just making a decision about that deal. I was establishing a cultural norm: truth matters more than winning. We don't build on dishonesty. We'd rather lose a deal than compromise our integrity. That principle became part of how that team operated. Even after I left, people would reference that moment: "Remember when Justin stopped the sales pitch to correct the lies? That's who we are."

Culture is built slowly, through consistent decisions over time. Once it's built, it has momentum. It shapes how people think, how they make decisions, how they treat each other. That's generational impact. That's leaving an inheritance to your children's children. Not money, but a way of operating that outlasts you.

Measuring Success by Fruit, Not Flash

The corporate world measures success by metrics that can be reported quarterly. Revenue growth. Market share. Productivity gains. Efficiency improvements. Those things matter. I'm not anti-metrics (quite the opposite), but they're not the full picture.

> **Matthew 7:16-20** *"You will recognize them by their fruits. Are grapes gathered from thornbushes, or figs from thistles? So, every healthy tree bears good fruit, but the diseased tree bears bad fruit. A healthy tree cannot bear bad fruit, nor can a diseased tree bear good fruit. Every tree that does not bear good fruit is cut down and thrown into the fire. Thus you will recognize them by their fruits."*

Fruit. Not flash. Not immediate results. Fruit, which takes time to grow. What's the fruit of your leadership? Not this quarter, but over years? Are the people you've led better for having been on your team? Have they grown? Have they become leaders themselves? Is the culture healthier because of your influence? More honest? More grace-filled?

More committed to doing what's right even when it's hard? Are the decisions you've made building something that will last or are you just optimizing for numbers that will be forgotten in three months? Those are fruit questions and fruit takes time.

The Long Obedience in the Same Direction

> There's a phrase I've come to love: "A long obedience
> in the same direction."
> Friedrich Nietzshe, popularized by Eugene Peterson

That's the long view. Not dramatic transformations. Not quarterly breakthroughs. Just consistent faithfulness, over time, moving in the same direction.

> **Hebrews 12:1** *"Therefore, since we are surrounded by*
> *so great a cloud of witnesses, let us also lay aside every*
> *weight, and sin which clings so closely, and let us run*
> *with endurance the race that is set before us."*

Endurance. Not speed. Not quarterly sprints. Endurance. The leaders I most respect aren't the ones who had one amazing quarter. They're the ones who've been faithful for decades. Who've built something that lasts. Who've maintained their principles under pressure, over and over, year after year. That's the long view and it's the only view that matters if you're trying to build something that outlasts you.

The Cost of the Long View

I'm not going to pretend the long view is easy or cost-free. Taking the long view often means accepting short-term pain. It means telling your boss, "I know you want these numbers, but compromising to get them will cost us more in the long run." It means making decisions that look bad on this quarter's report but are right for the long-term health of the organization.

Sometimes, that costs you. You miss targets. You get pressure from above. You might even lose your job if you're too committed to principles in an organization that only cares about short-term results. I've felt that pressure. I've had bosses who didn't understand why I wouldn't just do whatever it took to hit the numbers. I've been in meetings where I was the only one arguing for the long-term view and everyone else thought I was being naively idealistic.

It's lonely sometimes, and costly. Here's the thing: the cost of the short view is always greater. When you compromise principles for short-term gain, you might get immediate results, but you lose something more important. Trust. Credibility. Integrity. The foundation you're trying to build on. Once you lose that, it's almost impossible to get back.

The billing mistake taught me that. The short-term thinking cost us everything we were trying to protect. The damage to my own sense of integrity, the knowledge that I'd compromised when I shouldn't have, that cost was greater than any quarterly number could ever compensate for.

Making Decisions for the Long Term

So how do you actually make decisions for the long term when the pressure is always short-term?

Here's what I try to do:

1. Ask what this decision looks like in five years

When I'm facing pressure to compromise, I try to project forward: If I make this decision, what does the outcome look like in five years? Not this quarter. Five years. Will I be glad I made this decision? Will the thing I'm trying to protect actually be protected, or will the compromise undermine it? That long-term projection often clarifies whether the short-term gain is worth it.

2. Identify which principles are non-negotiable

I've learned to be clear with myself (and with leadership above me) about which principles I won't compromise, no matter the pressure. Truth. Integrity. Treating people with dignity. Those are non-negotiable for me. I'll find creative solutions, I'll accept short-term pain, but I won't compromise those. Other things are negotiable. I can flex on timelines, on strategies, on tactics. The principles that define who I am and who I want to be? Those don't change based on quarterly pressure.

3. Trust that faithfulness compounds

This is the hardest one, because it requires faith that you won't see the results immediately. Over and over, I've seen that faithfulness to principles, even when it's costly short-term, compounds over time.

It builds trust. It builds credibility. It builds a reputation that opens doors you didn't even know existed.

The junior analyst situation? That decision built trust across my entire team. That trust paid dividends in ways I couldn't have predicted. The sales meeting? That honesty built a relationship that lasted years and brought in far more revenue than that one deal would have. Faithfulness compounds, but you have to be patient enough to see it.

The Secular Translation

If you're not tracking with the Biblical language, here's the business case: short-term thinking destroys long-term value. Organizations that optimize for quarterly earnings at the expense of long-term health often see initial gains followed by eventual collapse. Enron. World-Com. Wells Fargo's fake accounts scandal. All examples of short-term thinking destroying long-term value.

Meanwhile, organizations that build on long-term principles, even when it costs them short-term, tend to outlast their competitors. They build cultures people want to work for. They develop reputations that attract the best talent and the best clients. They weather storms that destroy less principled competitors.

The research backs this up: companies led by leaders with long-term orientation outperform those led by short-term thinkers. Not every quarter, but over decades. The long view isn't just morally right. It's strategically sound.

What I'm Still Learning

I don't always get this right. There are times when I've given in to short-term pressure when I should have held firm. Times when I've optimized for the quarter when I should have held to principle. I'm learning, and the older I get, the more convinced I become that the long view is the only view that matters.

At the end of my career, no one's going to remember what my numbers were in Q3 of 2019. I don't even remember that. People will remember how I treated them. What kind of culture I built. Whether I led with integrity or compromised for convenience. That's legacy, and legacy is measured in decades, not quarters.

If you take nothing else from this chapter, take this: The pressure to optimize for the short term is constant, but building anything that lasts requires the long view. Principles hold under pressure. Short-term thinking collapses under pressure.

Build on rock, even if it takes longer. When the storm comes, and it always comes, you want to be standing on something that holds. Not something that looked impressive for a few quarters and then fell apart. That's the difference between flash and fruit. Between quarterly results and lasting legacy. Between sand and rock.

Choose the long view. Build on principle. Accept the short-term costs. Trust that in due season, if you don't give up, you'll reap what you've sown. You will. Every time.

The Tested
Framework

I didn't set out to write a book about Biblical leadership. I set out to make sense of eighteen years of experience, most of it learned the hard way. Bad bosses who taught me what not to do. Failures that forced me to reconsider how I thought about people and pressure. Decisions made under fire that either held up or fell apart.

The framework I built came from the wreckage. From watching leaders destroy trust and deciding I wouldn't lead that way. From making mistakes and having to figure out how to do better. From trial and error, crisis and consequence, over nearly two decades.

Then I became a Christian, and I started reading Scripture seriously. I kept finding my framework showing up in the Bible. Not because I'd been trying to be Biblical, but because I'd been trying to be *true*. It turns out those are the same thing. That's the premise of this entire book: good principles aren't good because they're Christian. They're Christian because they're good. They describe reality accurately because they work when you test them under pressure and that's how God designed them! That means they work whether you believe in the Bible or not.

The Framework, One More Time

If you've made it this far, you've seen this framework applied dozens of times in dozens of situations. Let me state it clearly one more time, because this is what I want you to take with you:

1. Humility: Check your motives and blind spots

Before you make a decision about someone else, ask yourself: Have I ever done what they just did? What am I missing about this situation? Am I judging them more harshly than I'd want to be judged? This isn't weakness. It's wisdom. The moment you think you're above someone else's failure is the moment you become most vulnerable to it yourself.

> **Galatians 6:1** *"Brothers, if anyone is caught in any transgression, you who are spiritual should restore him in a spirit of gentleness. Keep watch on yourself, lest you too be tempted."*

Keep watch on yourself. Humility isn't just about how you treat others. It's about recognizing your own capacity for failure.

2. Whole Counsel: Understand complete impact

Don't make decisions based on incomplete information. See the whole person, not just the failure. Understand the whole situation, not just the surface problem.

What's going on in their life that might explain this behavior? What are the systemic factors that contributed to this outcome? What will the full consequences be, human and business, if I make this decision?

> **Proverbs 18:13** *"If one gives an answer before he hears, it is his folly and shame."*

Hear the whole story before you decide. Context changes everything.

3. Restoration or Protection: Fix when possible, defend when necessary

When someone fails, the first question should always be: Can this be fixed? Can this person be restored? If the answer is yes, if they're remorseful and the failure was honest, invest in restoration. Grace isn't just kind, it's strategic. People who experience grace become loyal and improve.

If the answer is no, if the pattern is persistent and people are being harmed, protection becomes necessary. Grace for the person causing harm can't come at the expense of the people being harmed.

Both are expressions of the same principle: people matter. Sometimes that means investing in their growth. Sometimes that means defending those they're hurting. Galatians 6:2 *"Bear one another's burdens."* But Ezekiel 34:4 condemns leaders who don't protect the vulnerable. Both are true. Discernment is knowing which the moment requires.

4. Moral Intuition: Shaped by principles, not politics

At the end of the day, after you've considered humility and context and whether restoration or protection is needed, you have to ask: Does this feel right?

Not "Will this make people happy?" Not "Is this politically expedient?" Does this align with what's true and good and just? That moral intuition isn't something you manufacture in the moment. It's shaped over time by the principles you've internalized. By what you've chosen to value, what you've chosen to pursue, what you've chosen to become.

> **Romans 12:2** "...transformed by the renewal of your mind."

That transformation changes your intuition. What feels right to you changes as your mind is shaped by truth. When that intuition is aligned with what's actually true, it becomes a reliable guide under pressure.

Why This Works

Here's why this framework has held up for me across hundreds of decisions in dozens of contexts: It's not based on feelings. Feelings change. Pressure changes. Circumstances change. Principles hold.

It's not based on outcomes. You can't always control outcomes. Sometimes you make the right decision and things still go badly. You can control whether you made the decision based on principle or convenience.

It's based on truth. On what's actually real about people, about trust, about how change happens, about justice and mercy and wisdom. Truth doesn't change based on context. It's true in healthcare and tech and finance and government. It's true with employees and clients and vendors and executives. It's true when you're a junior developer and when you're a CTO.

That's why it works and that's why it will keep working. Reality doesn't change. Principles that accurately describe reality will always produce better outcomes than approaches that ignore it.

For Christian Leaders

If you're reading this as a Christian, here's my challenge to you:

Stop compartmentalizing your faith and your work.

You don't have "spiritual you" and "work you." You're one person, and your faith should shape how you see *everything*, not just "religious" things. Let Biblical principles inform your decision-making. Not by quoting Scripture in every meeting, but by letting Scripture shape how you think about people, about failure, about justice, about mercy, about truth.

Be the kind of person that makes people curious about your faith.

Not by talking about it constantly, but by living in a way that's different enough, compelling enough, that people want to understand where it comes from. The junior analyst never asked me if I was a Christian, but she experienced the fruit of a Biblical framework. The women who reported harassment never needed to know I read the Bible every morning, but they benefited from a leadership approach shaped by what the Bible says about protecting the vulnerable. That's integration. That's witness. That's what it means to let your light shine (Matthew 5:16).

When people do ask, when your leadership creates enough curiosity that they want to know where it comes from, be ready. With gentleness and respect. Not with a sermon, but with an honest explanation of how your faith shapes your framework.

Build for the long term.

The corporate world operates on quarterly cycles. The Kingdom of God operates on generational timelines. Don't let short-term pressure cause you to compromise long-term principles. Build on rock, even when sand would be faster. When the storm comes, and it always comes, you want to be standing on something that holds.

For Secular Leaders

If you're reading this as someone who doesn't share my faith, here's what I want you to know:

These principles work whether you're Christian or not.

You don't have to believe in the Bible to recognize that humility produces better decisions than arrogance. You don't have to pray to understand that grace often accomplishes more than punishment. You don't have to be religious to see that truth builds trust and lies destroy it.

These principles work because they align with reality. They're descriptions of how people actually function, how trust is actually built, how change actually happens.

3,000 years of tested wisdom has something to say about your Tuesday meeting.

The Bible isn't just ancient religious text. It's a collection of wisdom tested across millennia, across cultures, across every kind of human situation you can imagine. Some of that wisdom directly applies to the leadership challenges you're facing right now.

You don't have to accept the theological framework to benefit from the practical wisdom. You can test these principles in your own context and see if they hold up. I think you'll find that they do. Not because they're Christian, but because they're true.

Character-driven leadership produces better results.

Not always immediately. Not every quarter, but over time, leaders who operate from principle outperform leaders who operate from convenience. People want to work for leaders they can trust. Clients want to do business with companies that have integrity. Investors increasingly recognize that long-term value is built on culture and character, not just quarterly earnings.

The business case for principled leadership is strong. It's getting stronger as people become more selective about who they work for and what organizations they support. You don't need my faith to lead this way. You just need to be committed to building on what's true instead of what's expedient.

The Challenge

Whether you're a Christian or not, here's what I'm asking you to do:

Build your own framework.

Don't just borrow mine. Test these principles in your own context. Adapt them. Refine them. Make them yours. The specifics might look different for you. The language might be different, but the core principles, humility, whole counsel, restoration or protection, moral intuition shaped by truth, those should translate.

Test it under pressure.

Frameworks are easy to believe in when everything's going well. The test is whether they hold when the pressure's on. When you're facing a crisis. When your job's on the line. When the easy path and the right path diverge. That's when you find out whether your principles are real or just words you say when it's convenient.

Be willing to admit rough edges.

You're not going to get this right all the time. I haven't. I've got three whole chapters in this book about the ways I still struggle (I could have written hundreds more), the areas where I still fail, and the tensions I'm still working through. That's not failure. That's honesty, and honesty about your limitations is more valuable than pretending you've arrived.

Keep growing.

> **Philippians 1:6** *"And I am sure of this, that he who began a good work in you will bring it to completion at the day of Christ Jesus."*

If you're a Christian, God's not done with you yet. You're still being shaped. Still being refined. Still growing. If you're not a Christian, the principle still applies: you're not a finished product. You're still learning. Still developing. Still becoming the leader you want to be. Don't let the gap between who you are and who you want to be discourage you. Let it motivate you to keep pressing forward.

The Promise

Here's what I can promise you if you commit to building your leadership on principles that are true:

- **You'll have principles that hold when feelings don't.**

Feelings change. Pressure comes and goes. Circumstances shift, but if your framework is built on what's true, it will hold when everything else is unstable. You won't have to second-guess every decision. You won't have to wonder if you did the right thing. You'll know you led according to principle, and you can stand on that even when the outcome isn't what you hoped.

- **You'll build leadership that works because it's true.** Not because it's popular. Not because it's easy. Because it aligns with reality, and reality rewards those who work with it instead of against it. People will trust you. Not immediately, maybe, but over time, because consistency over time builds credibility, and credibility is the foundation of influence.

- **You'll create a reputation built on consistency.** Not perfection. Consistency. A pattern of behavior, over time, that teaches people what to expect from you. That reputation will open doors you didn't know existed. Will create opportunities you couldn't have manufactured. Will give you influence that goes far beyond your title or your position. People want to follow leaders they can trust. Trust is built in a thousand small decisions that prove, over and over, that your principles hold when the pressure's on.

The End, and the Beginning

This is the end of the book. But it's just the beginning of the work. The question isn't whether you agree with everything I've written. The question is: What are you going to do with it?

Are you going to test these principles in your own context? Adapt them? Refine them? Build on them?

Are you going to lead according to what's true, even when it's hard? Even when it costs you? Even when no one's watching?

Are you going to build on rock, knowing it takes longer but holds when the storm comes?

That's the challenge. That's the opportunity. That's the invitation. Not to be perfect, but to be faithful. To lead according to principle, not convenience. To build something that lasts, not just something that looks good this quarter. The framework is tested. The principles are true. The question is: will you use them?

I hope you will.

Not because I need you to validate my approach, but because the world needs leaders who've been shaped by truth. Who lead according to what's right, not just what's expedient. Who build on rock instead of sand.

Christian or not, that kind of leadership is desperately needed. You can be that kind of leader. Starting today. Starting with the next decision you make. Starting with the next person you lead. The tested framework is here. The principles hold. Now go build something that lasts.

Appendices

Appendix A: The Four-Part Framework - Quick Reference

This is the framework you can return to when decisions get hard, when pressure mounts, and when the right path isn't obvious.

The Four Questions

1. HUMILITY: Who Am I to Judge? What Am I Missing?

Before you decide what to do about someone else, check yourself.
Ask:

- Have I ever made this same mistake?

- Am I judging them more harshly than I'd want to be judged?

- What blind spots might I have about this situation?

- Is my ego clouding my judgment?

- What am I not seeing?

Biblical Foundation:
- Galatians 6:1 - "Keep watch on yourself, lest you too be tempted"

- Proverbs 11:2 - "With the humble is wisdom"

- James 4:6 - "God opposes the proud but gives grace to the humble"

Why It Matters: Pride blinds you to your own limitations. Humility creates space for wisdom to come from anywhere, including the person who just failed.

2. WHOLE COUNSEL: What's the Complete Human and Business Impact?

Don't make decisions based on incomplete information.
   Ask:
- What's the whole story, not just the surface problem?

- Who else does this affect?

- What are the human consequences, not just business outcomes?

- What systemic factors contributed to this situation?

- What will happen to everyone involved if I make this decision?

Biblical Foundation:

- Proverbs 18:13 - "If one gives an answer before he hears, it is his folly and shame"

- Proverbs 31:8-9 - "Defend the rights of the poor and needy"

Why It Matters: Decisions based on partial information are decisions made with blindfolds on. Context changes everything.

3. RESTORATION OR PROTECTION: Can This Be Fixed, or Does Someone Need Defending?

When someone fails, discern which the moment requires.
Ask:
Can this person be restored?

- Is this an honest mistake or a pattern of harm?

- Are they remorseful and willing to change?

- Are other people being hurt by this behavior?

- Does grace serve restoration here, or does it enable harm?

- Who am I really protecting with my decision?

Biblical Foundation:
- Galatians 6:1-2 - "Restore him in a spirit of gentleness. Bear one another's burdens"

- Galatians 6:5 - "Each will have to bear his own load"

- Matthew 18:15-17 - Process of restoration with boundaries

- Ezekiel 34:4 - Condemnation for leaders who don't protect

the vulnerable

Why It Matters: Grace and accountability aren't opposites. Both matter. Wisdom is knowing which the situation requires.

4. MORAL INTUITION: Does This Feel Right Based on Principles, Not Politics?

After considering humility, context, and restoration or protection, ask your gut.
   Ask:

- Does this align with what's true, good, and just?

- Am I choosing this because it's right, or because it's convenient?

- Would I be proud to explain this decision publicly?

- Is this based on principle, or am I rationalizing?

- What does my gut say when I strip away the pressure and politics?

Biblical Foundation:

- Romans 12:2 - "Be transformed by the renewal of your mind, that by testing you may discern what is the will of God"

- Proverbs 3:5-6 - "Trust in the Lord... and he will make straight your paths"

Why It Matters: Moral intuition shaped by tested principles is a reliable guide when everything else is unstable. But intuition not grounded in truth is just feelings.

How to Use This Framework

This isn't a formula. You can't plug in variables and get an answer. It's a way of thinking through complex decisions when the easy path and the right path diverge.

Work through the questions in order:

1. Start with humility (check your motives and blind spots)

2. Gather whole counsel (understand complete impact)

3. Determine restoration or protection (what does the situation require?)

4. Test against moral intuition (does this align with principle?)

The framework works by:

- Slowing you down when pressure demands quick reactions

- Forcing clarity when emotions cloud judgment

- Grounding decisions in principle when politics pulls you toward convenience

- Creating consistency over time that builds trust

When the framework breaks: Usually it's not the framework that fails, it's you (or me). We know what's right, but we choose convenience, politics, or self-protection instead.

When that happens, the framework still proves itself by showing what gets destroyed when you violate it. (See Chapter 9: The $350,000 billing mistake)

Quick Decision Guide

Copy this page, laminate it, keep it at your desk, or in your wallet.

BEFORE YOU DECIDE:

- **HUMILITY:** Have I checked my motives and blind spots? Am I missing something?

- **WHOLE COUNSEL:** Do I understand the complete human and business impact?

- **RESTORATION OR PROTECTION:** Can this be fixed, or does someone need defending?

- **MORAL INTUITION:** Does this feel right based on principles, not politics?

WHEN YOU'RE TEMPTED TO COMPROMISE:

- Will I be able to defend this decision six months from now?

- Am I choosing this because it's right, or because it's convenient?

- What am I really protecting: the principle or myself?

AFTER YOU DECIDE:

- Did I apply the framework, or did I rationalize around it?

- Can I explain my reasoning based on principle, not just outcome?

- If this decision turns out badly, can I stand on the process I used?

For Christian Leaders

This framework works because it aligns with how God designed reality to function. The principles aren't arbitrary, they're descriptive. They describe how trust is actually built, how people actually change, how justice and mercy actually intersect.

Your job isn't to make your leadership "Christian" by quoting Scripture in meetings. It's to let Biblical truth shape how you see everything, then lead so well that people wonder where it comes from.

When they ask, you'll be ready (1 Peter 3:15).

For Secular Leaders

This framework works whether you believe the Bible or not. Test it in your own context. Adapt it. Refine it. See if it holds under pressure.

These aren't religious platitudes. They're principles forged in crisis, refined through failure, proven under real pressure with real consequences.

You don't have to pray to recognize that humility produces better decisions than arrogance. You don't have to go to church to see that understanding whole counsel leads to wiser outcomes. You don't have to believe in God to observe that grace often accomplishes more than punishment.

Truth works. Every time. Whether you believe in the source or not.

Common Scenarios

Someone makes a catastrophic mistake:

1. Humility: Have I ever made a big mistake? How would I

want to be treated?

2. Whole Counsel: What's their track record? What's at stake for them personally?

3. Restoration or Protection: Is this a first offense or a pattern? Can they learn from this?

4. Moral Intuition: Does grace here build loyalty or enable carelessness?

Someone causes persistent harm:

1. Humility: Am I avoiding action because it's hard, or because it's truly unclear?

2. Whole Counsel: Who's being hurt? What happens if I do nothing?

3. Restoration or Protection: Have I tried restoration? Is protection now necessary?

4. Moral Intuition: Am I protecting the vulnerable or protecting my comfort?

You're pressured to compromise integrity:

1. Humility: Why am I tempted? What am I really protecting?

2. Whole Counsel: What gets destroyed if I compromise? What if the truth comes out?

3. Restoration or Protection: Does short-term convenience destroy long-term trust?

4. Moral Intuition: Can I stand on this decision when it's dis-

covered?

A high performer is toxic to the team:

1. Humility: Am I protecting them because they're valuable or because I'm afraid to act?

2. Whole Counsel: What's the cost to everyone else? What message does tolerance send?

3. Restoration or Protection: Can their behavior be fixed? Are others being harmed?

4. Moral Intuition: Is keeping them worth destroying trust with everyone else?

The Promise

If you use this framework consistently, over time:

- **You'll have principles that hold when feelings don't.** Pressure changes, circumstances shift, but the framework remains steady.

- **You'll make better decisions.** Not perfect ones, but decisions you can stand on when outcomes aren't what you hoped.

- **You'll build trust over time.** Consistency over time creates credibility. Credibility becomes influence.

- **You'll create a reputation built on principle.** People will trust you with what matters most, because they've watched you make hard calls based on what's right, not what's expedient.

The framework is tested. The principles are true. The question is: will you use them?

Appendix B: Interview Questions That Test Character

Most interviews test competence. These questions test character. Because competence is the baseline, character is the multiplier.

The Two-Directional Ego Test

Based on Chapter 10, this is the core method for detecting ego and testing teachability in interviews.

The Setup

1. **Have a technical or strategic discussion** about a real challenge relevant to the role

2. **Ask them to propose a solution** and walk through their reasoning

3. **Propose an alternative approach** (sometimes worse, sometimes better, sometimes just different)

4. **Watch what happens next**

What You're Actually Testing

Test #1: How do they react when challenged?
- Do they get defensive or stay open?

- Do they make excuses or genuinely consider the alternative?

- Does their tone get harder or remain collaborative?

- Do they dismiss your suggestion in a way that makes you feel stupid?

Test #2: How do they react when they're right?
- Do they gloat subtly or stay focused on the problem?

- Do they explain your mistake condescendingly or guide you gently?

- Do they make you feel dumb or like you're collaborating?

- Do they need to win or do they need truth?

Red Flags (Don't Hire)

When Challenged:
- Body language shifts to defensive (crossed arms, narrowed eyes, tense posture)

- Voice gets harder, faster, more insistent

- They double down on clearly flawed ideas

- They dismiss your input without genuine consideration

- They make you feel stupid for disagreeing

When Right:
- Smile smugly or look pleased they caught the CTO's mistake

- Laugh like they just won something

- Explain why you're wrong in a way that feels condescending

- Spend five minutes enjoying their teaching moment

- Make you feel talked down to

Green Flags (Strong Hire)

When Challenged:

- Stay curious instead of defensive

- Ask clarifying questions about your approach

- Genuinely consider the alternative

- Disagree respectfully if they still think their way is better

- Make you feel like you're solving a problem together

When Right:

- Stay serious and focused on solving the problem

- Gently explain the flaw without rubbing it in

- Guide you to why their solution is better without condescension

- Move forward without celebrating their correctness

- Make you feel like a valued collaborator, not a student

Specific Questions That Reveal Character

Questions About Failure

"Tell me about a time you made a significant mistake at work. What happened, and how did you handle it?"
   What you're listening for:
   - Do they actually admit a real mistake, or minimize it?

   - Do they blame others or take ownership?

   - What did they learn from it?

   - Do they show humility about their capacity for failure?

   Red flags:
   - Can't think of a significant mistake (everyone has them)

   - The "mistake" is actually a humble-brag ("I worked too hard")

   - They blame circumstances or other people entirely

   - No evidence of learning or growth

   Green flags:
   - Admits a genuine failure honestly

   - Takes ownership without making excuses

   - Shows specific learning and change in behavior

   - Displays humility about their own limitations

"Tell me about a time you were wrong about something significant and someone else was right. How did you handle it?"

What you're listening for:

- Can they admit being wrong publicly?

- How did they treat the person who was right?

- Did they change course, or dig in?

- What does this reveal about their ego?

Red flags:

- Can't think of an example (everyone is wrong regularly)

- Minimize how wrong they were or how right the other person was

- Focus on why their thinking was reasonable given what they knew

- No evidence they changed their approach

Green flags:

- Admits being clearly wrong without defensiveness

- Credits the other person generously

- Changed course quickly once they saw the truth

- Shows they value truth over being right

Questions About Conflict

"Tell me about a time you disagreed with your manager about a significant decision. What happened?"

What you're listening for:

- Do they have the courage to speak up?

- How do they handle disagreement with authority?

- Can they disagree respectfully?

- What happened to the relationship afterward?

Red flags:

- Never disagreed with a manager (either lying or spineless)

- The story reveals they were combative or insubordinate

- They're still bitter about it

- They badmouth their former manager

Green flags:

- Respectfully raised concerns with specific reasoning

- Made their case without being combative

- Either changed their mind when given more context, or the manager changed course

- Relationship remained strong regardless of outcome

- Shows respect for authority while maintaining conviction

"Tell me about a time you had to give difficult feedback to someone. How did you approach it?"

What you're listening for:

- Can they have hard conversations?

- How do they handle being right when it requires correcting someone?

- Do they avoid confrontation or lean into it with grace?

Red flags:
- Avoided giving the feedback and the situation got worse

- Gave feedback in a way that was harsh or demeaning

- Focused on making the person feel bad rather than helping them improve

- No evidence of care for the person's growth

Green flags:
- Prepared thoughtfully for the conversation

- Delivered truth with kindness and clarity

- Focused on helping the person improve, not just correcting

- Followed up to support change

- Maintained the relationship through the difficult conversation

Questions About Working with Others

"Tell me about a time you worked with someone whose approach was very different from yours. How did you handle it?"

What you're listening for:

- Can they work with people who think differently?

- Do they value diversity of thought or just people who agree with them?

- Are they collaborative or controlling?

Red flags:

- They tried to change the person to work their way

- They couldn't find value in the different approach

- The story reveals frustration with anyone who doesn't think like them

- No evidence of learning from the experience

Green flags:

- Sought to understand the different approach

- Found ways to leverage both approaches

- Learned something from the collaboration

- Values cognitive diversity as strength, not obstacle

"Tell me about a time you had to trust someone with something important even though you had doubts. What happened?"

What you're listening for:

- Can they delegate and trust others?

- How do they handle risk when they're not in control?

- Do they micromanage or empower?

Red flags:
- They didn't actually trust, they just monitored closely

- The story reveals they swooped in at the first sign of trouble

- They can't delegate without hovering

- No evidence they learned to trust better

Green flags:
- Actually let go and trusted the person

- Supported without micromanaging

- Person either succeeded (validating trust) or failed (learning opportunity)

- Shows they can empower others even when it's uncomfortable

Questions About Values

"Tell me about a time you had to choose between what was right and what was expedient. What did you choose and why?"
What you're listening for:
- Do they have a moral compass?

- Have they actually faced ethical dilemmas?

- How do they make decisions when pressure is high?

Red flags:

- Can't think of a time (everyone faces these choices)

- Chose expediency and justify it extensively

- No evidence of principle-driven decision-making

- They seem proud of gaming the system

Green flags:

- Admits the choice was hard

- Chose what was right even at personal cost

- Can articulate the principle that guided them

- Shows consistency between stated values and actual behavior

"What do you do when you see someone being treated unfairly, but speaking up might cost you politically?"
What you're listening for:

- Will they protect vulnerable people?

- Do they have courage or just political savvy?

- What do they actually value when it costs them?

Red flags:

- Always stay silent to protect themselves

- Haven't actually stood up for anyone

- Calculate political cost before doing what's right

- No evidence of sacrificial advocacy

Green flags:

- Have actually spoken up at personal cost

- Show they value protecting vulnerable people over political safety

- Did it with wisdom (not just impulsive heroism)

- Would do it again despite the cost

Questions About Growth

"What's the hardest feedback you've ever received, and what did you do with it?"

What you're listening for:

- Can they receive hard truth?

- Do they get defensive or get better?

- Do they value growth over comfort?

Red flags:

- Can't think of hard feedback (everyone gets it)

- Disagree with the feedback and explain why it was wrong

- Didn't change anything as a result

- Still bitter about it

Green flags:

- Admits it was hard to hear

- Took time to process and accept it

- Changed behavior as a result

- Grateful for it in retrospect

- Shows they value truth over comfort

"Tell me about something you believed strongly five years ago that you've changed your mind about. What changed?"
What you're listening for:

- Are they intellectually flexible?

- Can they update their beliefs based on new information?

- Do they dig in or adapt?

Red flags:

- Can't think of anything they've changed their mind about

- The change was trivial (not a real belief)

- Defensive about why they believed it in the first place

- No evidence of intellectual humility

Green flags:

- Changed mind about something significant

- Can explain what new information or experience shifted their thinking

- Not defensive about having been wrong

- Shows they value truth over consistency

The Strategic Vulnerability Move

In the interview, explicitly admit when the candidate is right and you're wrong.

Why This Works

1. **Tests their character:** How do they handle victory?
2. **Models the culture:** Shows how you actually treat each other
3. **Builds trust:** Demonstrates you'll admit mistakes after they're hired

What to Say

"You know what? You're right. I'm absolutely wrong on that. Good catch."

Then watch. Their response tells you everything you need to know about how they'll behave when they have the advantage.

Red Flags vs. Yellow Flags

Red Flags (Don't Hire)

- Can't admit real mistakes

- Blame others consistently

- Condescending when right

- Defensive when challenged

- No evidence of growth from feedback

- Haven't changed their mind about anything significant

- Never stood up for anyone at personal cost

- Badmouth former managers or colleagues

Yellow Flags (Probe Deeper)

- Give "safe" examples that don't reveal much

- Seem overly polished in answers (rehearsed)

- Avoid taking strong positions

- Focus too much on process, not enough on principle

- Difficulty with self-assessment

- Haven't faced significant challenges

The 80% Success Rate

This process isn't foolproof. About 20% of people will fool you for 60 minutes. They'll say the right things, show the right body language, and pass your tests.

But 80% is way better than hiring on credentials and technical skills alone.

When You Miss

Go back and review:

- What subtle red flags did you miss?

- What questions could have revealed this sooner?

- How can you refine what you're watching for?

Every miss is a learning opportunity to get slightly better at detecting character.

What Gentle Correction Actually Sounds Like

Bad Correction (Ego):
- "Yeah, that won't work because..." [makes it obvious you should have known]

- "I actually thought about that approach, but it's got some pretty serious problems"

- [Laughs] "I mean, you *could* do that, but..."

- [Five-minute lecture on why you're wrong]

Good Correction (Humble Strength):
- "I think that might run into issues with [constraint]. How would that handle [specific problem]?"

- "That's interesting. One concern I have is [flaw]. How would that work?"

- "I see what you're going for. We'd need to consider [flaw], which might make [my approach] more reliable"

- "Good question. The main issue I see is [flaw]. If we could solve that, your approach might work, but [alternative] might be simpler"

Questions to Ask Yourself After the Interview

- How did I feel during the interview? Talked down to or collaborated with?

- Did they make me feel dumb when they were right?

- Did they get defensive when challenged?

- Would I want to work with this person during a crisis at 2 AM?

- Did they show humility about their own limitations?

- Did they show grace when they had the advantage?

- Would they make the team better or just be individually productive?

- Do they value truth over ego?

For Christian Leaders

These questions test for Biblical character traits:

    1. **Humility** (James 4:6)

    2. **Teachability** (Proverbs 12:1)

    3. **Grace under advantage** (Philippians 2:3)

    4. **Wisdom over ego** (Proverbs 12:15)

You're hiring people who can operate within the four-part framework, who'll reinforce the culture you're building, who value truth over politics.

For Secular Leaders

These questions test for universal character traits:

- Can they learn?

- Can they collaborate?

- Do they have integrity?

- Will they make the team better?

Skills can be taught. Character under pressure reveals who someone is when things get hard.

Hire accordingly.

Sample Interview Flow

Phase 1: Build Rapport (10 minutes) - Get them comfortable - Talk through their background - Create conversational environment

Phase 2: Technical/Strategic Discussion (20 minutes) - Present real scenario - Ask for their approach - Engage in collaborative problem-solving - **Deploy the two-directional ego test**

Phase 3: Character Questions (20 minutes) - Pick 3-4 questions from this appendix - Ask follow-up questions to go deeper - Listen for patterns, not just stories

Phase 4: Close (10 minutes) - Answer their questions - Explain next steps - Thank them for their time

After: - Debrief immediately while impressions are fresh - Answer the self-assessment questions - Make decision based on character + competence, not just skills

The Ultimate Test

Would you trust this person with something that matters, when no one is watching, when getting it wrong would cost you significantly?

If the answer is no, don't hire them.

If the answer is yes, you've found someone worth building with.

Appendix C: Biblical Leadership Principles - Cross-Reference

For Christian leaders who want to study the Biblical foundation of the framework more deeply. Organized by theme with chapter references.

The Four-Part Framework in Scripture

1. Humility

"Who am I to judge? What am I missing?"

Galatians 6:1 (ESV) - *"Brothers, if anyone is caught in any transgression, you who are spiritual should restore him in a spirit of gentleness. Keep watch on yourself, lest you too be tempted."* - Check yourself before judging others - Referenced in: Introduction, Chapter 5

Proverbs 11:2 (ESV) - *"When pride comes, then comes disgrace, but with the humble is wisdom."* - Pride blinds, humility clarifies - Referenced in: Chapter 5

James 4:6 (ESV) - *"God opposes the proud but gives grace to the humble."* - The stakes of pride vs. humility - Referenced in: Chapters 5, 10

Proverbs 26:12 (ESV) - *"Do you see a man who is wise in his own eyes? There is more hope for a fool than for him."* - The danger of thinking you've arrived - Referenced in: Chapter 10

Proverbs 12:15 (ESV) - *"The way of a fool is right in his own eyes, but a wise man listens to advice."* - Teachability as wisdom - Referenced in: Chapter 10

Philippians 3:12 (ESV) - *"Not that I have already obtained this or am already perfect, but I press on to make it my own, because Christ Jesus has made me his own."* - Paul models ongoing growth - Referenced in: Chapter 17

Proverbs 16:18 (ESV) - *"Pride goes before destruction, and a haughty spirit before a fall."* - The inevitable consequence of pride

James 1:19 (ESV) - *"Let every person be quick to hear, slow to speak, slow to anger."* - The posture of humility in action

2. Whole Counsel

"What's the complete human and business impact?"

Proverbs 18:13 (ESV) - *"If one gives an answer before he hears, it is his folly and shame."* - Don't decide on incomplete information - Referenced in: Introduction, Conclusion, Chapter 5

Proverbs 31:8-9 (ESV) - *"Open your mouth for the mute, for the rights of all who are destitute. Open your mouth, judge righteously, defend the rights of the poor and needy."* - Consider impact on the vulnerable - Referenced in: Chapter 5

Proverbs 18:17 (ESV) - *"The one who states his case first seems right, until the other comes and examines him."* - Always hear multiple perspectives

Proverbs 15:22 (ESV) - *"Without counsel plans fail, but with many advisers they succeed."* - Gather wisdom from multiple sources

1 Kings 3:16-28 - *The wisdom of Solomon* - Understanding full context reveals truth - The famous story of two mothers

Proverbs 25:2 (ESV) - *"It is the glory of God to conceal things, but the glory of kings is to search things out."* - Leaders must investigate, not assume

3. Restoration or Protection

"Can this be fixed, or does someone need defending?"

Galatians 6:1-2 (ESV) - *"Brothers, if anyone is caught in any transgression, you who are spiritual should restore him in a spirit of gentleness. Keep watch on yourself, lest you too be tempted. Bear one another's burdens, and so fulfill the law of Christ."* - Restoration with gentleness - Referenced in: Introduction, Chapter 5, Conclusion

Galatians 6:5 (ESV) - *"For each will have to bear his own load."* - But also accountability - Referenced in: Chapter 5, Conclusion

Matthew 18:15-17 (ESV) - *"If your brother sins against you, go and tell him his fault, between you and him alone. If he listens to you, you have gained your brother. But if he does not listen, take one or two others along with you... If he refuses to listen even to the church, let him be to you as a Gentile and a tax collector."* - Process: restoration first, then boundaries - Referenced in: Chapter 5

Ezekiel 34:4 (ESV) - *"The weak you have not strengthened, the sick you have not healed, the injured you have not bound up, the strayed you have not brought back, the lost you have not sought, and with force and harshness you have ruled them."* - Condemnation for leaders who don't protect - Referenced in: Introduction, Chapter 5, Conclusion

Proverbs 24:11-12 (ESV) - *"Rescue those who are being taken away to death; hold back those who are stumbling to the slaughter. If you say, 'Behold, we did not know this,' does not he who weighs the heart perceive it?"* - You're accountable for protecting when you have power

James 5:19-20 (ESV) - *"My brothers, if anyone among you wanders from the truth and someone brings him back, let him know that whoever brings back a sinner from his wandering will save his soul from death and will cover a multitude of sins."* - The value of restoration when possible

2 Thessalonians 3:14-15 (ESV) - *"If anyone does not obey what we say in this letter, take note of that person, and have nothing to do with him, that he may be ashamed. Do not regard him as an enemy, but warn him as a brother."* - Boundaries without hatred

4. Moral Intuition

"Does this feel right based on principles, not politics?"

Romans 12:2 (ESV) - *"Do not be conformed to this world, but be transformed by the renewal of your mind, that by testing you may discern what is the will of God, what is good and acceptable and perfect."* - Transformed mind leads to reliable discernment - Referenced in: Introduction, Chapter 5, Conclusion

Proverbs 3:5-6 (ESV) - *"Trust in the Lord with all your heart, and do not lean on your own understanding. In all your ways acknowledge him, and he will make straight your paths."* - Intuition grounded in God, not just feelings - Referenced in: Chapter 5

Hebrews 5:14 (ESV) - *"But solid food is for the mature, for those who have their powers of discernment trained by constant practice to distinguish good from evil."* - Moral intuition is trained over time

Proverbs 23:23 (ESV) - *"Buy truth, and do not sell it; buy wisdom, instruction, and understanding."* - Value truth at cost to self - Referenced in: Chapter 10

Philippians 1:9-10 (ESV) - *"And it is my prayer that your love may abound more and more, with knowledge and all discernment, so that you may approve what is excellent, and so be pure and blameless for the day of Christ."* - Discernment develops through love shaped by knowledge

Leadership Principles by Theme

Trust and Integrity

Proverbs 28:13 (ESV) - *"Whoever conceals his transgressions will not prosper, but he who confesses and forsakes them will obtain mercy."* - Hiding mistakes destroys trust - Referenced in: Chapter 9 (The $350,000 billing mistake)

Numbers 32:23 (ESV) - *"But if you will not do so, behold, you have sinned against the Lord, and be sure your sin will find you out."* - Truth always surfaces - Referenced in: Chapter 9

Proverbs 12:22 (ESV) - *"Lying lips are an abomination to the Lord, but those who act faithfully are his delight."* - Integrity matters to God

Proverbs 11:3 (ESV) - *"The integrity of the upright guides them, but the crookedness of the treacherous destroys them."* - Integrity as reliable guide

Proverbs 10:9 (ESV) - *"Whoever walks in integrity walks securely, but he who makes his ways crooked will be found out."* - Security in honesty

Psalm 15:1-2, 4 (ESV) - *"O Lord, who shall sojourn in your tent? Who shall dwell on your holy hill? He who walks blamelessly and does what is right and speaks truth in his heart... who swears to his own hurt and does not change."* - Keep your word even when it costs you - Referenced in: Chapter 4 (trust breaker)

Grace and Mercy

Matthew 18:21-22 (ESV) - *"Then Peter came up and said to him, 'Lord, how often will my brother sin against me, and I forgive him?*

As many as seven times?' Jesus said to him, 'I do not say to you seven times, but seventy-seven times.'" - Extend grace repeatedly - Referenced in: Chapter 6 (QA analyst)

Luke 6:36 (ESV) - *"Be merciful, even as your Father is merciful."* - Model God's mercy

Ephesians 4:32 (ESV) - *"Be kind to one another, tenderhearted, forgiving one another, as God in Christ forgave you."* - Grace as reflection of gospel

Micah 6:8 (ESV) - *"He has told you, O man, what is good; and what does the Lord require of you but to do justice, and to love kindness, and to walk humbly with your God?"* - The balance: justice AND kindness

Matthew 5:7 (ESV) - *"Blessed are the merciful, for they shall receive mercy."* - What you extend, you receive

Authority and Leadership

1 Peter 5:2-3 (ESV) - *"Shepherd the flock of God that is among you, exercising oversight, not under compulsion, but willingly, as God would have you; not for shameful gain, but eagerly; not domineering over those in your charge, but being examples to the flock."* - How to exercise authority rightly - Referenced in: Chapter 1 (email hacker)

Matthew 20:25-28 (ESV) - *"You know that the rulers of the Gentiles lord it over them, and their great ones exercise authority over them. It shall not be so among you. But whoever would be great among you must be your servant, and whoever would be first among you must be your slave, even as the Son of Man came not to be served but to serve, and to give his life as a ransom for many."* - Servant leadership model - Referenced in: Chapter 1

Ephesians 6:9 (ESV) - *"Masters, do the same to them, and stop your threatening, knowing that he who is both their Master and yours is in*

heaven, and that there is no partiality with him." - Leaders answer to God - Referenced in: Chapter 1

Proverbs 29:2 (ESV) - *"When the righteous increase, the people rejoice, but when the wicked rule, the people groan."* - Leadership impact on culture

Proverbs 16:12 (ESV) - *"It is an abomination to kings to do evil, for the throne is established by righteousness."* - Authority sustained by righteousness

Wisdom and Counsel

Proverbs 27:17 (ESV) - *"Iron sharpens iron, and one man sharpens another."* - Value of mutual challenge - Referenced in: Chapter 10

Proverbs 11:14 (ESV) - *"Where there is no guidance, a people falls, but in an abundance of counselors there is safety."* - Seek multiple perspectives

Proverbs 13:10 (ESV) - *"By insolence comes nothing but strife, but with those who take advice is wisdom."* - Humility as path to wisdom

Proverbs 19:20 (ESV) - *"Listen to advice and accept instruction, that you may gain wisdom in the future."* - Teachability matters

Proverbs 12:1 (ESV) - *"Whoever loves discipline loves knowledge, but he who hates reproof is stupid."* - Strong language about rejecting feedback - Referenced in: Chapter 10

Character Under Pressure

Philippians 2:3 (ESV) - *"Do nothing from selfish ambition or conceit, but in humility count others more significant than yourselves."* - How to handle having the advantage - Referenced in: Chapters 10, Introduction

1 Timothy 3:3 (ESV) - *"[An overseer must be] not violent but gentle, not quarrelsome, not a lover of money."* - Character qualifications for leaders - Referenced in: Chapter 10

Proverbs 15:1 (ESV) - *"A soft answer turns away wrath, but a harsh word stirs up anger."* - Gentleness as strength - Referenced in: Chapter 10

Ephesians 4:29 (ESV) - *"Let no corrupting talk come out of your mouths, but only such as is good for building up, as fits the occasion, that it may give grace to those who hear."* - Speech that builds, not tears down - Referenced in: Chapter 10

James 1:19-20 (ESV) - *"Know this, my beloved brothers: let every person be quick to hear, slow to speak, slow to anger; for the anger of man does not produce the righteousness of God."* - Anger doesn't produce righteousness

Justice and Protection

Isaiah 1:17 (ESV) - *"Learn to do good; seek justice, correct oppression; bring justice to the fatherless, plead the widow's cause."* - Leaders protect the vulnerable

Psalm 82:3-4 (ESV) - *"Give justice to the weak and the fatherless; maintain the right of the afflicted and the destitute. Rescue the weak and the needy; deliver them from the hand of the wicked."* - God's call to defend the defenseless

Proverbs 21:15 (ESV) - *"When justice is done, it is a joy to the righteous but terror to evildoers."* - Justice creates safety

Amos 5:24 (ESV) - *"But let justice roll down like waters, and righteousness like an ever-flowing stream."* - Justice as constant, not occasional

Zechariah 7:9-10 (ESV) - *"Thus says the Lord of hosts, Render true judgments, show kindness and mercy to one another, do not oppress the widow, the fatherless, the sojourner, or the poor, and let none of you devise evil against another in your heart."* - Justice, mercy, and protection together

Witness and Integration

1 Peter 3:15 (ESV) - *"But in your hearts honor Christ the Lord as holy, always being prepared to make a defense to anyone who asks you for a reason for the hope that is in you; yet do it with gentleness and respect."* - Live in a way that creates curiosity, then explain - Referenced in: Chapter 17, Conclusion

Matthew 5:16 (ESV) - *"In the same way, let your light shine before others, so that they may see your good works and give glory to your Father who is in heaven."* - Works create witness - Referenced in: Chapter 17, Conclusion

Colossians 3:23-24 (ESV) - *"Whatever you do, work heartily, as for the Lord and not for men, knowing that from the Lord you will receive the inheritance as your reward. You are serving the Lord Christ."* - Work as worship - Referenced in: Chapter 16

Titus 2:7-8 (ESV) - *"Show yourself in all respects to be a model of good works, and in your teaching show integrity, dignity, and sound speech that cannot be condemned, so that an opponent may be put to shame, having nothing evil to say about us."* - Character as apologetic

Truth and Reality

John 14:6 (ESV) - *"Jesus said to him, 'I am the way, and the truth, and the life. No one comes to the Father except through me.'"* - Jesus as embodiment of truth

    John 8:32 (ESV) - *"And you will know the truth, and the truth will set you free."* - Truth liberates

    Psalm 119:160 (ESV) - *"The sum of your word is truth, and every one of your righteous rules endures forever."* - God's Word as reliable truth

    Proverbs 16:9 (ESV) - *"The heart of man plans his way, but the Lord establishes his steps."* - God's sovereignty over our plans - Referenced in: Introduction

    Proverbs 21:2 (ESV) - *"Every way of a man is right in his own eyes, but the Lord weighs the heart."* - Self-justification vs. God's assessment - Referenced in: Chapter 10

Common Grace and General Revelation

Romans 1:20 (ESV) - *"For his invisible attributes, namely, his eternal power and divine nature, have been clearly perceived, ever since the creation of the world, in the things that have been made. So they are without excuse."* - God reveals truth through creation itself - Foundation for how an atheist can discover Biblical principles - Referenced in: Chapter 5

    Romans 2:14-15 (ESV) - *"For when Gentiles, who do not have the law, by nature do what the law requires, they are a law to themselves, even though they do not have the law. They show that the work of the law is written on their hearts, while their conscience also bears witness."* - Moral knowledge accessible apart from Scripture - Why the framework worked before faith - Referenced in: Chapter 5

Acts 14:17 (ESV) - *"Yet he did not leave himself without witness, for he did good by giving you rains from heaven and fruitful seasons, satisfying your hearts with food and gladness."* - God's goodness visible to all

Jesus as Leadership Model

How Jesus Handled Authority

John 8:1-11 - *Woman caught in adultery* - Had moral high ground, chose grace - "Go and sin no more" (truth + gentleness) - Referenced in: Chapter 10

John 4:1-26 - *Samaritan woman at the well* - Knew her whole history, didn't humiliate her - Offered living water instead of condemnation - Referenced in: Chapter 10

John 21:15-19 - *Peter's restoration* - Peter had denied Him, Jesus restored him - "Feed my sheep" (restoration over punishment) - Referenced in: Chapter 10

Mark 10:42-45 - *Leadership as service* - Contrasted with worldly power - "For even the Son of Man came not to be served but to serve"

Luke 22:24-27 - *Dispute about greatness* - "Let the greatest among you become as the youngest" - Servant leadership modeled

Study by Chapter

Introduction - By the Grace of God, They Aligned

- Galatians 6:1 (humility)

- Proverbs 18:13 (whole counsel)

- Galatians 6:2 & Ezekiel 34:4 (restoration/protection)

- Romans 12:2 (moral intuition)

- Proverbs 16:9 (God's sovereignty)

Chapter 1 - The Email Hacker

- 1 Peter 5:2-3 (not domineering)

- Ephesians 6:9 (stop threatening)

- Matthew 20:25-28 (servant leadership)

- Genesis 1-2, Matthew 25, John 15:15, Luke 10 (trust-based leadership)

Chapter 5 - The Pattern in the Pain

- All framework verses (see above)

- Romans 1:20, Romans 2:14-15 (common grace)

Chapter 9 - What Happens When You Violate the Framework

- Proverbs 28:13 (confession vs. concealment)

- Numbers 32:23 (sin will find you out)

- James 1:22 (doers, not just hearers)

Chapter 10 - Hiring for Character

- Proverbs 12:15, 26:12 (teachability)

- Philippians 2:3 (humility)

- 1 Timothy 3:3 (gentle, not quarrelsome)

- Proverbs 15:1 (soft answer)

- Ephesians 4:29 (building up)

- Proverbs 27:17 (iron sharpens iron)

- Proverbs 23:23 (buy truth)

- John 8, John 4, John 21 (Jesus handling advantage)

Chapter 17 - When They Ask

- 1 Peter 3:15 (prepared to give answer)

- Philippians 3:12 (not yet perfect)

- Matthew 5:16 (let your light shine)

Conclusion - The Tested Framework

- Summary of all framework verses

- Philippians 1:6 (God's work continues)

For Deeper Study

Books of the Bible Most Referenced

Proverbs - Practical wisdom about character, decision-making, leadership **Galatians** - Balance of grace and accountability **Gospels** (especially John) - Jesus' leadership model **1 Peter** - Christian behavior in secular contexts **Philippians** - Humility, service, transformation

Themes to Explore

- **The Wisdom Literature** (Proverbs, Ecclesiastes, Job) - How ancient wisdom applies to modern leadership

- **Paul's Qualifications for Leaders** (1 Timothy 3, Titus 1) - Character requirements for authority

- **Jesus' Interactions with People** - How He handled having advantage, power, and moral authority

- **The Prophets on Justice** (Isaiah, Amos, Micah) - God's heart for protecting the vulnerable

- **Common Grace** (Romans 1-2, Acts 14, 17) - How truth is accessible to all people

Cross-Reference Approach

When you read a chapter, keep this appendix nearby. Look up the verses referenced. Read them in context. See how they connect to the leadership principle being taught.

Don't just read the verse, read the surrounding passage. Biblical wisdom is deep, and you'll find more the more you dig.

Warning

Don't prooftext. Don't rip verses out of context to justify whatever you want to do. These principles work because they align with the full counsel of Scripture, not because isolated verses support them.

If a leadership decision contradicts the character of God revealed in Scripture, it's wrong. Period. Even if you can find a verse that seems to support it.

Always ask: Does this align with who God is? How Jesus led? What Scripture consistently teaches about character?

That's the grid. Use it.

Appendix D: Discussion Guide

This guide is designed for teams, book clubs, church small groups, or leadership cohorts studying this book together. Use it to facilitate meaningful conversations about integrating these principles into your leadership.

How to Use This Guide

For Study Groups

- **Duration:** 6-8 weeks (can be adapted)

- **Format:** 60-90 minute discussions

- **Group Size:** 4-10 people works best

- **Materials:** Everyone should read the assigned chapters before meeting

For Leadership Teams

- **Context:** Use during team off-sites, professional development, or regular leadership meetings

- **Focus:** Apply the framework to actual decisions you're facing

- **Goal:** Build shared language and shared principles for decision-making

For Church Groups

- **Context:** Small groups, men's/women's groups, marketplace ministry groups

- **Focus:** Integration of faith and work

- **Goal:** Help Christians lead with Biblical wisdom in secular contexts

Discussion Ground Rules

1. **Confidentiality:** What's shared in the room stays in the room

2. **Honesty:** This only works if people are real about struggles and failures

3. **No fixing:** Listen to understand, not to solve everyone's problems

4. **Equal participation:** Everyone speaks, no one dominates

5. **Assume good intent:** Give grace when people are working through hard ideas

6. **Apply to yourself first:** Focus on your own growth before critiquing others

Six-Week Study Plan

Week 1: The Framework's Foundation

Read: Introduction + Chapters 1-5 (Part 1: The Education of Pain)

Week 2: Grace and Protection

Read: Chapters 6-9 (Part 2: The Framework in Action, first half)

Week 3: Building the Culture

Read: Chapters 10-12 (Part 3: Building the Culture)

Week 4: The Rough Edges

Read: Chapters 13-15 (Part 4: The Rough Edges)

Week 5: The Integrated Life

Read: Chapters 16-18 (Part 5: The Integrated Life)

Week 6: Application and Commitment

Read: Conclusion + Review Framework

Week 1: The Framework's Foundation

Chapters: Introduction, Chapters 1-5

Opening Question (5 minutes)

What's the worst boss you've ever had, and what did they teach you about leadership (even if accidentally)?

Key Concepts to Discuss (30 minutes)

1. **The Four-Part Framework** Which of the four parts (Humility, Whole Counsel, Restoration/Protection, Moral Intuition) comes most naturally to you? - Which is hardest for you? - Give an example of when you've applied one of these (or failed to).

2. **Discovering Truth Without Faith** - How do you react to the idea that an atheist can discover Biblical principles through experience? - What does this say about truth and how God reveals Himself? - Have you seen secular leaders operate according to Biblical principles without knowing it?

3. **Bad Boss Lessons** - What patterns did you notice across the four bad boss stories (Chapters 1-4)? - Which bad boss do you most relate to? (Be honest - we all have failure modes) - What's one behavior you want to make sure you never replicate?

Personal Reflection Questions (20 minutes)

For Everyone: - When have you led from surveillance instead of trust? - When has your ego kept you from admitting you were wrong? - When have you been absent when presence mattered? - When have you broken confidence and destroyed trust?

Pick ONE to share with the group: Don't try to share all of them. Pick the one that hit hardest and be honest about it.

Application (15 minutes)

This Week's Practice: Before making any significant decision about people: 1. Check your humility: What am I missing? 2. Gather whole counsel: What's the full story? 3. Determine restoration or protection: What does this require? 4. Test moral intuition: Does this feel right for the right reasons?

Accountability: Share with one person in the group how you'll apply this.

Week 2: Grace and Protection

Chapters: 6-9

Opening Question (5 minutes)

Tell about a time someone extended grace to you when you deserved judgment. What impact did that have?

Key Concepts to Discuss (30 minutes)

1. **The QA Analyst Story (Chapter 6)** - Would you have extended grace in that situation? Why or why not? - What's the difference between grace and enabling? - How do you discern when to invest in restoration?

2. **The Inappropriate Employee (Chapter 7)** - At what point did restoration become insufficient and protection necessary? - How do you balance grace for the person failing with protection for those being harmed? - Have you ever kept someone too long when protection was needed? What happened?

3. **The Sales Meeting (Chapter 8)** - When has integrity cost you something significant? - How do you handle the pressure to compromise when the stakes are real? - What makes it hard to choose truth when convenience is available?

4. **The Billing Mistake (Chapter 9)** - Why do you think the author included a story where he failed? - What's the

difference between a story where the framework works and a story where violating it proves it by negative example? - When have you rationalized your way into a bad decision?

Personal Reflection Questions (20 minutes)

Restoration: - Who have you given up on too quickly? - Who should you have invested in longer?

Protection: - Who have you kept too long while others were being harmed? - When have you prioritized the wrong person's comfort over someone else's safety?

Integrity: - When have you compromised and regretted it? - When have you chosen integrity at cost and been glad you did?

Pick ONE to share: Again, go deep on one rather than surface-level on all.

Application (15 minutes)

This Week's Practice:

Identify one person on your team or in your life: - **Option 1:** Someone who needs restoration - what would investing in them look like? - **Option 2:** Someone you've kept too long - what would protection require? - **Option 3:** An area where you're tempted to compromise - how will you choose integrity?

Pick ONE. Don't try to do all three. Go deep on one decision.

Week 3: Building the Culture

Chapters: 10-12

Opening Question (5 minutes)

What's the best team culture you've ever been part of? What made it great?

Key Concepts to Discuss (30 minutes)

1. **Hiring for Character (Chapter 10)** - How does the two-directional ego test work? - Have you ever hired someone brilliant who destroyed the team? What happened? - What would change if you tested for character as rigorously as you test for skills?

2. **Collaborative Decision-Making (Chapter 11)** - How do you involve people in decisions without it becoming "design by committee"? - When have you made a better decision because someone challenged you? - When have you shut down good input and regretted it?

3. **Reputation (Chapter 12)** - What do people say about you when you're not in the room? - How do small decisions compound into reputation over time? - What's one behavior you need to change because it's inconsistent with who you want to be?

Personal Reflection Questions (20 minutes)

Hiring: - Think about your last few hires. Did you test for character or just competence? - Who on your team do you wish you'd interviewed more carefully?

Decision-Making: - Are you open to being challenged, or do people fear disagreeing with you? - When was the last time someone changed your mind? What does that tell you?

Reputation: - Are there areas where your private behavior doesn't match your public values? - What would people who watch you closely say you truly value?

Application (15 minutes)

This Week's Practice:
Choose ONE:

1. **Next interview:** Use the two-directional ego test. Deliberately admit when the candidate is right and watch their response.

2. **Next decision:** Invite challenge. Explicitly ask someone to push back on your thinking and genuinely consider their input.

3. **Daily behaviors:** Identify one small behavior you'll change to align your reputation with your values.

Week 4: The Rough Edges

Chapters: 13-15

Opening Question (5 minutes)

What's your biggest rough edge as a leader? The thing you're still working on?

Key Concepts to Discuss (30 minutes)

1. **When Frustration Wins (Chapter 13)** - When are you most likely to become the leader you don't want to be? - What triggers your frustration? Incompetence? Slow progress? Repeated mistakes? - How do you lead differently when you're frustrated vs. when you're centered?

2. **Written-Off People (Chapter 14)** - Who have you written off? Why? - Is it wisdom or pride that keeps you from receiving from them? - When has someone you dismissed turned out to be right about something?

3. **The Favorites Problem (Chapter 15)** - Do you have favorites? Be honest. - What's the difference between appropriate trust and inappropriate favoritism? - How do you audit whether you're being fair?

Personal Reflection Questions (20 minutes)

This week is about honesty, not performance. The author admits these are areas he's still working on. So should you.

Frustration: - When was the last time you lost your temper or said something you regretted? - What patterns do you notice in when you become someone you're not proud of?

Written-Off: - Who have you stopped listening to? - Is it because they've proven unwise, or because they challenged you once and you didn't like it?

Favorites: - Name your favorites. Why are they favorites? - Is it because of their character and competence, or because they make your life easier?

You don't have to share all of these. Pick the one that hit hardest.

Application (15 minutes)

This Week's Practice:

1. **Identify your trigger**- What situations make you frustrated? Can you build a pattern-interrupt for when you feel it coming?

2. **Reconsider someone you've written off** - Listen to them. Actually listen. See if there's wisdom you've been missing.

3. **Audit your favorites**- Are you giving opportunities based on merit or comfort? Make one decision this week based on principle, not preference.

Pick the practice that addresses your biggest rough edge.

Week 5: The Integrated Life

Chapters: 16-18

Opening Question (5 minutes)

How integrated is your faith and your work? Be honest - are you compartmentalized or integrated?

Key Concepts to Discuss (30 minutes)

1. **Beyond Sunday Morning (Chapter 16)** - What does compartmentalized faith look like? - What changes when you let Biblical principles shape how you actually work? - Where are you still keeping faith and work separate?

2. **When They Ask (Chapter 17)** - Has anyone ever asked you about your faith because of how you lead? - What would need to change for your leadership to create that kind of curiosity? - How do you balance not hiding faith but not being pushy?

3. **The Long View (Chapter 18)** - How does thinking in decades instead of quarters change leadership decisions? - What are you building that will outlast your tenure? - What matters more: this quarter's results or trust that compounds over years?

Personal Reflection Questions (20 minutes)

Integration: Where is there a gap between your Sunday faith and your Monday leadership? - What Biblical principle do you believe but not practice at work? - What would change if you fully integrated your faith?

Witness: Are you worth asking about? Would your leadership make someone curious about where it comes from? - What's keeping you from being more open about your faith? Fear? Wisdom? Shame?

Legacy: What do you want to be known for in 20 years? - Are your current decisions building toward that or away from it? - What would you change if you led for legacy instead of quarterly results?

Application (15 minutes)

This Week's Practice:

1. **For Christians:** Identify ONE area where you're compartmentalized and practice integration. Let a Biblical principle shape an actual decision.

2. **For Everyone:** Lead in a way this week that might make someone curious. Practice the 1 Peter 3:15 approach: live in a way worth asking about, then be ready.

3. **Long view:** Make ONE decision this week based on what builds long-term trust instead of short-term wins.

Week 6: Application and Commitment

Read: Conclusion + Review the Framework (Appendix A)

Opening Question (5 minutes)

What's the one thing from this book that hit you hardest? The thing you know you need to change?

Review: The Tested Framework (20 minutes)

Go through each part of the framework as a group. For each one, share:
1. **Humility** - When did you see this work in the book? In your life?

2. **Whole Counsel** - What changes when you gather complete information before deciding?

3. **Restoration or Protection** - What's one situation where you now see which was needed?

4. **Moral Intuition** - How has your moral intuition been shaped by this study?

Personal Commitments (20 minutes)

Each person shares (briefly):
1. **One principle** you're committing to apply

2. **One behavior** you're committing to change

3. **One person** who will hold you accountable

This shouldn't be a laundry list. Pick ONE thing in each category and go deep.

Group Discussion (20 minutes)

For Christian Leaders: - How will this change how you integrate faith and work? - What will you do differently starting Monday? - How will you be ready when people ask?

    For Secular Leaders: - Which principles are you committing to test? - How will you adapt the framework to your context? - What's the first decision you'll apply this to?

    For Teams: - What shared language did we gain from this study? - How will we hold each other accountable to these principles? - What decision process will we use going forward?

Closing Exercise (10 minutes)

Write this down:

"The one thing I'm changing because of this book is..."

"I'll know I've successfully changed this when..."

"The person who will hold me accountable is..."

Share with one other person in the group. Check in with each other in 30 days.

Ongoing Application

Monthly Check-In Questions

After finishing the study, revisit these monthly:

1. **Am I applying the framework consistently or selectively?**

2. **What decision did I make this month that tested my principles?**

3. **Where did I compromise, and why?**

4. **Where did I hold to principle at cost?**

5. **What rough edges am I still working on?**

6. **Is my leadership creating curiosity about where it comes from?**

Annual Framework Review

Once a year, work through the framework assessment:

Humility: Do I regularly check my blind spots before making decisions? □ Can I admit when I'm wrong without defensiveness? □ Do I create space for wisdom to come from anyone?

Whole Counsel: Do I gather complete information before deciding? □ Do I consider impact on all stakeholders, especially vulnerable ones? □ Do I understand context before judging?

Restoration or Protection: Do I default to restoration when appropriate? □ Do I protect people when harm is continuing? □ Can I discern which the situation requires?

Moral Intuition: Do my decisions align with principles or just convenience? □ Can I defend my reasoning based on what's right? □ Would I be proud to explain my decisions publicly?

For Facilitators

How to Lead These Discussions

1. **Create safety** - Model vulnerability by going first - Don't let anyone dominate - Protect confidentiality fiercely

2. **Go deep, not wide** - Better to discuss one concept thoroughly than skim several - When someone shares something real, sit with it - Don't rush to solve or fix

3. **Connect to real situations** - Use actual decisions people are facing - Make it practical, not just theoretical - "How would the framework apply to [specific situation]?"

4. **Hold space for disagreement** - Not everyone will agree with everything - That's okay and actually valuable - Learn to disagree well

5. **End with application** - Every session should end with "What will you do differently?" - Build in accountability - Follow up on commitments

Dealing with Difficult Dynamics

Someone dominates: "I want to hear from people who haven't spoken yet."

Someone is defensive: "This is hard stuff. We're all learning. No judgment."

Someone criticizes the book: "What about that bothers you? Let's discuss it."

Silence when you ask a question: "Let's take 60 seconds to think about that individually, then share."

Surface-level answers: "Can you go deeper on that? What's underneath that?"

Adaptations for Different Groups

For Executive Teams

- Focus on strategic decisions and organizational culture

- Use the framework to make actual decisions during the study

- Commit to shared language and shared principles

- Hold each other accountable as peers

For Church Small Groups

- Emphasize Biblical foundation (use Appendix C)

- Focus on witness and integration

- Connect to discipleship and spiritual formation

- Support each other in living faith at work

For Cross-Functional Teams

- Use common language from the book

- Focus on how different roles apply the framework

- Build trust through vulnerability about failures

- Create shared culture across departments

For Marketplace Ministry

- Mix Christians and non-Christians

- Show how principles work for everyone

- Create space for Christians to be ready (1 Peter 3:15)

- Demonstrate integration without being pushy

Additional Resources

If your group wants to go deeper:

1. **Use Appendix B** to practice interview techniques together

2. **Study Appendix C** for deeper Biblical foundation

3. **Bring real decisions** to the group and apply the framework together

4. **Invite guest speakers** who lead with these principles

5. **Do case studies** of decisions group members are actually facing

Final Encouragement

This study only works if you're honest. About failures. About rough edges. About the gap between who you are and who you want to be.

The goal isn't perfection. It's faithfulness. Leading according to principle instead of convenience. Building something that lasts instead of something that looks good this quarter.

The framework is tested. The principles are true. The question is: will you use them?

Not just for six weeks. But for a career. For a lifetime. For a legacy.

Start with the next decision you make. Then the one after that. Then the one after that.

Over time, consistency becomes credibility. Credibility becomes trust. Trust becomes influence.

And influence creates opportunities to shape how others lead, which multiplies your impact far beyond anything you could accomplish alone.

That's what this study is for. Not just to learn principles, but to become leaders worth following.

Go build something that lasts.

Appendix E: Leadership Self-Assessment Tool

Use this tool quarterly to evaluate how consistently you're applying the framework. Be brutally honest, this only helps if you're real with yourself.

How to Use This Assessment

Frequency: Every 3 months (quarterly)

Process: 1. Block 60-90 minutes of uninterrupted time 2. Review each section honestly 3. Score yourself on each question (1-5 scale) 4. Identify patterns and commitments 5. Share results with one accountability partner 6. Revisit your commitments next quarter

Scoring: - **1** = Never/Rarely - **2** = Occasionally - **3** = Sometimes - **4** = Usually - **5** = Consistently

The goal isn't a perfect score. The goal is honest assessment and intentional growth.

Part 1: Humility Assessment

Self-Awareness

Before making significant decisions about people, I check my own capacity for the same failure. □ 1 □ 2 □ 3 □ 4 □ 5

I actively seek out perspectives that challenge my assumptions. □ 1 □ 2 □ 3 □ 4 □ 5

I regularly ask "What am I missing?" before concluding I'm right. □ 1 □ 2 □ 3 □ 4 □ 5

I can admit when I'm wrong without getting defensive. □ 1 □ 2 □ 3 □ 4 □ 5

I change my mind when presented with better information. □ 1 □ 2 □ 3 □ 4 □ 5

Teachability

When someone challenges my thinking, my first response is curiosity, not defensiveness. □ 1 □ 2 □ 3 □ 4 □ 5

I actively invite people to tell me where I'm wrong. □ 1 □ 2 □ 3 □ 4 □ 5

I've changed course on something significant in the last quarter based on someone else's input. □ 1 □ 2 □ 3 □ 4 □ 5

I see correction as a gift, not a threat. □ 1 □ 2 □ 3 □ 4 □ 5

People feel safe challenging me without fear of retaliation. □ 1 □ 2 □ 3 □ 4 □ 5

Pride Check

I don't need to be the smartest person in the room. □ 1 □ 2 □ 3 □ 4 □ 5

I can celebrate when someone else has a better idea than mine. □ 1 □ 2 □ 3 □ 4 □ 5

I don't feel threatened when someone on my team gets recognition. □ 1 □ 2 □ 3 □ 4 □ 5

I acknowledge my limitations publicly and appropriately. □ 1 □ 2 □ 3 □ 4 □ 5

I default to "I might be wrong" rather than "I'm probably right." □ 1 □ 2 □ 3 □ 4 □ 5

HUMILITY SECTION SCORE: _____/75

Part 2: Whole Counsel Assessment

Information Gathering

I gather complete information before making decisions about people. □ 1 □ 2 □ 3 □ 4 □ 5

I seek multiple perspectives, not just confirmation of what I already think. □ 1 □ 2 □ 3 □ 4 □ 5

I ask "What's really going on here?" instead of accepting surface explanations. □ 1 □ 2 □ 3 □ 4 □ 5

I understand the full human and business impact before deciding. □ 1 □ 2 □ 3 □ 4 □ 5

I don't make snap judgments based on partial information. □ 1 □ 2 □ 3 □ 4 □ 5

Considering Impact

I think through who will be affected by my decisions, not just the immediate parties. □ 1 □ 2 □ 3 □ 4 □ 5

I consider long-term consequences, not just short-term outcomes. □ 1 □ 2 □ 3 □ 4 □ 5

I pay attention to systemic factors, not just individual behavior. □ 1 □ 2 □ 3 □ 4 □ 5

I understand what's at stake for the people involved personally, not just professionally. □ 1 □ 2 □ 3 □ 4 □ 5

I ask questions to understand context before making conclusions. □ 1 □ 2 □ 3 □ 4 □ 5

Protecting the Vulnerable

I specifically consider impact on vulnerable or marginalized people. □ 1 □ 2 □ 3 □ 4 □ 5

I hear from people who might be afraid to speak up. □ 1 □ 2 □ 3 □ 4 □ 5

I don't just listen to the loudest voices or most powerful people. □ 1 □ 2 □ 3 □ 4 □ 5

I ask "Who doesn't have a voice in this conversation?" □ 1 □ 2 □ 3 □ 4 □ 5

I'm willing to make unpopular decisions to protect vulnerable people. □ 1 □ 2 □ 3 □ 4 □ 5

WHOLE COUNSEL SECTION SCORE: _____/75

Part 3: Restoration or Protection Assessment

Restoration Mindset

When someone fails, my first question is "Can this be fixed?" not "How do I punish this?" □ 1 □ 2 □ 3 □ 4 □ 5

I invest in people who show remorse and willingness to change. □ 1 □ 2 □ 3 □ 4 □ 5

I've seen grace produce loyalty and growth in people I've restored. □ 1 □ 2 □ 3 □ 4 □ 5

I create path back from failure when appropriate. □ 1 □ 2 □ 3 □ 4 □ 5

I distinguish between honest mistakes and patterns of harm. □ 1 □ 2 □ 3 □ 4 □ 5

Protection Mindset

When restoration isn't working, I protect people being harmed.
□ 1 □ 2 □ 3 □ 4 □ 5

I don't keep toxic people just because they're high performers.
□ 1 □ 2 □ 3 □ 4 □ 5

I act decisively when someone's pattern shows they won't change. □ 1 □ 2 □ 3 □ 4 □ 5

I prioritize safety of many over comfort of one when necessary. □ 1 □ 2 □ 3 □ 4 □ 5

I don't confuse grace with enabling harm. □ 1 □ 2 □ 3 □ 4 □ 5

Discernment

I can discern which the situation requires: restoration or protection. □ 1 □ 2 □ 3 □ 4 □ 5

I've given appropriate chances without giving infinite chances. □ 1 □ 2 □ 3 □ 4 □ 5

I act based on patterns, not isolated incidents. □ 1 □ 2 □ 3 □ 4 □ 5

I hold people accountable without being punitive. □ 1 □ 2 □ 3 □ 4 □ 5

I don't default to one approach (all grace or all accountability). □ 1 □ 2 □ 3 □ 4 □ 5

RESTORATION/PROTECTION SECTION SCORE: _____/75

Part 4: Moral Intuition Assessment

Principle Over Politics

I choose what's right over what's convenient. □ 1 □ 2 □ 3 □ 4 □ 5

I make decisions I can defend based on principle, not just outcome. □ 1 □ 2 □ 3 □ 4 □ 5

I don't compromise integrity under pressure. □ 1 □ 2 □ 3 □ 4 □ 5

Political consequences don't override moral clarity. □ 1 □ 2 □ 3 □ 4 □ 5

I'd be proud to explain my decisions publicly. □ 1 □ 2 □ 3 □ 4 □ 5

Truth Over Comfort

I tell the truth even when it costs me. □ 1 □ 2 □ 3 □ 4 □ 5

I don't hide mistakes or hope they won't be discovered. □ 1 □ 2 □ 3 □ 4 □ 5

I speak up when something's wrong, even when it's risky. □ 1 □ 2 □ 3 □ 4 □ 5

I don't rationalize my way into bad decisions. □ 1 □ 2 □ 3 □ 4 □ 5

I'm honest about my limitations and failures. □ 1 □ 2 □ 3 □ 4 □ 5

Alignment Check

My decisions align with my stated values. □ 1 □ 2 □ 3 □ 4 □ 5

I can point to the principle guiding my decisions. □ 1 □ 2 □ 3 □ 4 □ 5

I notice when something feels wrong and I investigate that feeling. □ 1 □ 2 □ 3 □ 4 □ 5

I don't override my moral intuition with rationalizations. □ 1 □ 2 □ 3 □ 4 □ 5

My leadership is consistent with who I say I am. □ 1 □ 2 □ 3 □ 4 □ 5

MORAL INTUITION SECTION SCORE: _____/75

Part 5: Trust and Culture Assessment

Psychological Safety

People feel safe disagreeing with me. □ 1 □ 2 □ 3 □ 4 □ 5

Team members admit mistakes without fear. □ 1 □ 2 □ 3 □ 4 □ 5

People come to me with problems before they become crises. □ 1 □ 2 □ 3 □ 4 □ 5

Bad news reaches me quickly because people trust how I'll respond. □ 1 □ 2 □ 3 □ 4 □ 5

I've created a culture where failure is a learning opportunity, not a firing offense. □ 1 □ 2 □ 3 □ 4 □ 5

Confidentiality and Trust

I keep confidence unless breaking it is necessary for protection. □ 1 □ 2 □ 3 □ 4 □ 5

People trust me with sensitive information. □ 1 □ 2 □ 3 □ 4 □ 5

I don't gossip or share information for political gain. □ 1 □ 2 □ 3 □ 4 □ 5

People know their vulnerability with me won't be weaponized. □ 1 □ 2 □ 3 □ 4 □ 5

I handle private information with appropriate gravity. □ 1 □ 2 □ 3 □ 4 □ 5

Freedom and Control

I trust people to do their jobs without micromanaging. □ 1 □ 2 □ 3 □ 4 □ 5

I delegate authority, not just tasks. □ 1 □ 2 □ 3 □ 4 □ 5

I lead from security, not insecurity. □ 1 □ 2 □ 3 □ 4 □ 5

I give people autonomy appropriate to their demonstrated competence. □ 1 □ 2 □ 3 □ 4 □ 5

I don't monitor people out of fear, I support them out of trust. □ 1 □ 2 □ 3 □ 4 □ 5

TRUST AND CULTURE SECTION SCORE: _____/75

Part 6: Character and Rough Edges Assessment

Emotional Regulation

I stay centered under pressure instead of reacting emotionally. □ 1 □ 2 □ 3 □ 4 □ 5

Frustration doesn't make me become a leader I'm not proud of. □ 1 □ 2 □ 3 □ 4 □ 5

I apologize when I lose my temper or say something I regret. □ 1 □ 2 □ 3 □ 4 □ 5

People would say I'm consistent, not moody or unpredictable. □ 1 □ 2 □ 3 □ 4 □ 5

I can delay my response until I'm thinking clearly. ☐ 1 ☐ 2 ☐ 3 ☐ 4 ☐ 5

Receiving Feedback

I receive feedback with curiosity, not defensiveness. ☐ 1 ☐ 2 ☐ 3 ☐ 4 ☐ 5

I actively seek feedback from people who see my blind spots. ☐ 1 ☐ 2 ☐ 3 ☐ 4 ☐ 5

I don't write people off just because they challenged me. ☐ 1 ☐ 2 ☐ 3 ☐ 4 ☐ 5

I value correction from anyone, not just people I already respect. ☐ 1 ☐ 2 ☐ 3 ☐ 4 ☐ 5

I've changed something significant because someone gave me hard feedback. ☐ 1 ☐ 2 ☐ 3 ☐ 4 ☐ 5

Fairness and Favoritism

I give opportunities based on merit, not personal preference. ☐ 1 ☐ 2 ☐ 3 ☐ 4 ☐ 5

I audit whether I'm being fair or just comfortable. ☐ 1 ☐ 2 ☐ 3 ☐ 4 ☐ 5

My "favorites" are people who've earned trust through character, not just people who don't challenge me. ☐ 1 ☐ 2 ☐ 3 ☐ 4 ☐ 5

People would say I treat everyone fairly regardless of personal rapport. ☐ 1 ☐ 2 ☐ 3 ☐ 4 ☐ 5

I'm honest with myself about partiality and work to correct it. ☐ 1 ☐ 2 ☐ 3 ☐ 4 ☐ 5

CHARACTER AND ROUGH EDGES SECTION SCORE: ____/75

Overall Scores

HUMILITY: ____/75 **WHOLE COUNSEL:** ____/75 **RESTORATION/PROTECTION:** ____/75 **MORAL INTUITION:** ____/75 **TRUST AND CULTURE:** ____/75 **CHARACTER:** ____/75
TOTAL SCORE: ____/450

Score Interpretation

- **360-450:** You're consistently applying the framework. Keep growing in weak areas.

- **270-359:** You're applying it often but have room for more consistency.

- **180-269:** You understand the principles but struggle with consistent application.

- **90-179:** You're beginning to apply the framework but need significant development.

- **Below 90:** Be honest, are you really applying these principles or just learning about them?

Remember: The goal isn't a perfect score. The goal is honest assessment and intentional growth.

Reflection Questions

After completing the assessment, answer these:

Where Am I Strong?

My highest-scoring section was: _____
   What I'm doing well:
   How I'll leverage this strength:

Where Am I Weak?

My lowest-scoring section was: _____
   Specific areas where I scored 1-2:
   Root causes (not just symptoms):

What Patterns Do I Notice?

Looking at my lowest scores, what theme emerges? (Fear? Pride?
Impatience? Conflict avoidance? People-pleasing? Control?)
   How does this pattern show up in my leadership?
   What's the cost of not addressing this?

Quarterly Commitments

This Quarter, I Will:

1. One Behavior I'll Change:
   Specific action:
   How I'll know I've changed:
   Who will hold me accountable:
   2. One Strength I'll Leverage:

How I'll use this to help others:

Where I'll apply this more intentionally:

3. One Rough Edge I'll Address:

The trigger I'll watch for:

The new response I'll practice:

The person who'll call me out:

Accountability Partner

Share this assessment with one trusted person who will: - Check in with you monthly - Call you out when you violate your commitments - Celebrate growth with you - Pray for you if you're a person of faith

My accountability partner for this quarter: _____

We will check in: (dates) _____, _____, _____

Next Quarter

Date for next assessment: _____

Set a calendar reminder now so you don't skip it.

When you complete next quarter's assessment: 1. Review this quarter's commitments first 2. Celebrate what changed 3. Be honest about what didn't 4. Set new commitments building on progress

For Christian Leaders

Add these reflection questions:

Am I leading in a way that reflects Christ?

Would my leadership make someone curious about my faith?

Am I integrating Biblical principles or just compartmental-izing?

Where is there a gap between my Sunday faith and Monday leadership?

What would God say about how I'm leading?

For Teams

If your leadership team does this together:

1.   **Share scores** (if you've built enough trust)
2.   **Identify team patterns** (not individual weaknesses)
3.   **Commit to one shared improvement**
4.   **Hold each other accountable**
5.   **Celebrate team growth**

Final Reminder

You are not your score.

This tool measures consistency, not character. We all have rough edges. We're all growing.

The question isn't "Am I perfect?" The question is "Am I growing?"

If your scores improve over time, you're doing the work.

If they stay the same or decline, investigate why. Are you being more honest? Or have you stopped trying?

The framework is tested. The principles are true. The question is: are you applying them?

This assessment helps you answer that honestly.

Now go lead in a way that builds something worth leaving behind.

www.ingramcontent.com/pod-product-compliance
Lightning Source LLC
Chambersburg PA
CBHW071950100426
42736CB00043B/2717